EVER THE OPTIMIST

GYLISA JAYNE

Chapter 1- The Decision

Adventure, I have come to realise, is not found following a map or scaling a mountain. Adventure isn't always a huge and notable thing. Sometimes adventure is just the mindset we go into, to tackle the small everyday obstacles in our lives...

It is a state of mind that opens us up to living life, as it *should* be lived. Throwing caution to the wind, and daring to be wild, for a while.

Adventure is simply the name of the process we go through to get from soul-crushing monotony, to something new. Something much more special.

Adventure happens when we stop hearing to what our brain thinks, to begin listening what our soul feels.

So, did I imagine spending my 21st birthday living out of car? Whilst my friends took trips to Vegas, had huge parties and gifts of house deposits. Um, no. I did not. It didn't seem fair, but well, I knew by then that life isn't fair sometimes.

We must take a leap when the opportunity arises.

And here we were, taking that leap...

And landing in a business estate somewhere near Plymouth.

******

'Life's unfair' Dad tells me.

Yes, Dad. I know.

He said it when he handed us our pocket money as kids, my twin brother Tom getting £13 and I would get £10. 'That's not fair.' I'd say, staring at the money in each our hands.

 'Life's not fair.' They'd both argue back.

He said it when I had to use his bank account for my wages, because I didn't have an account of my own. He would withdraw an amount he thought I'd earnt and keep whatever was left over. It didn't matter that it was all mine. I knew better than to argue. I knew what the answer would be.

Life was unfair.

Mum had moved out a few years before, as living with Dad had become difficult, although sometimes we would have a few days of clarity. The clouds would part from over the house and everything would feel light, and happy again.

Some days I'd bake a cake and we'd drink tea together and chat at the table. Other days he'd throw plates around and scream up the stairs. If we were really unlucky – and all of us were, at some point, we would arrive home to find our belongings strewn across the driveway.

 Dad did it to my sister first, until one day she didn't come back. Then to Mum, when I was 14. Two weeks before our school exams, I remember. I wondered if having your mum ejected from your house by your dad would garner any favours from my exam invigilators.

It did not.

I helped her organise some of the mess, 18 years of her life into bin bags, folding her clothes and fishing her jewellery out of the bushes.

'I'll come back for you.' She promised me, stuffing the bags into her car.

And then she was gone.

I hid our family life from everyone I could, silently understanding that some people don't see it if you don't want them to, and others won't see if even if you do. I soon realised; it wasn't the norm to find your bedrooms contents outside the front of the house when you bring friends back for tea.

My friends had Dads that would cook dinner and listen to what they did that day. Dads who had hobbies and never seemed to be around to cause the tension that filled our house to the brim. It seemed that there were people out there living entirely normal lives.

Dad had been that guy once, cycling to get a week's shop on his bike, worrying about us at home with Mum – who was suffering with severe post-natal depression. He read to us and drew a mural on my bedroom wall. He introduced us to music and encouraged us to draw and make things. We would pack picnics up and sit on the sandy banks of the river near our house, calling it our private beach. Childhood then seemed like a fairy tale.

But along the way, the years started getting harder. Dad began smoking more 'spliffs', and then drinking. His moods became erratic and volatile.

 Dysfunction became our new normal.

Now Ryan was here, Dad often seemed more volatile than ever, unable to deal with the loss of control he was feeling. He would demand to know what we'd be up to if he went out and would check the house for any signs of wrongdoing. I wasn't sure what he was looking for, he certainly never found it.

Life felt difficult, but equally like it wasn't really happening to me - so I just got on with it.

The simplest of things, like a tidy house, felt like luxury living to me. I'd marvel at my friends' houses, with cream (!) carpets or fresh laundry.

My best friend Hannah, would marvel at mine. We joked that we'd swapped lives by mistake, despite her being older than me. She loved that my house was full of battered antiques, and that 'anything goes.' Tom and I had spray painted his bedroom one afternoon, and got high off the fumes by mistake. Dad had got back and demanded to know what we were up to. When we'd sheepishly admitted we were 'tagging' our names on the ceiling, he called back up 'Open a fucking window then!'

I'd often make wishes on stars or the clock when it hit 11:11. I wish that tomorrow nothing awful happens. I wish for a good day today. I wish Dad is fine when I get back.

I should have been wishing for something more, but when your peace is held on a tiny string, it's hard to look any further than the next day.

It struck me then, that each day was slipping away as a total 'non-event.' That if I didn't do something now, I'd get to old age and be one of those people who thinks 'where did all those years go?'

I could feel that there was something more waiting for us, on the other side of – what? I wasn't sure.

But I felt it growing louder, every day on the commute to the office. It had begun as a murmur - Every morning as I discovered the cereal we'd bought had been eaten, again. When I returned from a long shift at work, I checked my bank and it said 'insufficient funds'. The murmur began to hum.

Slowly, I could make out the words. Pushing the thought away when I found myself doing the same month over, and then the same week. And then the same day. Until every day, my mind was screaming at me, 'There has to be more than this!'

I'd look around, wondering if my colleagues could hear the same chant. What was theirs saying? Or had it been so deeply buried by now it had silenced? Was I the only one?

It seemed that everyone around me was happy with their lot. The most interesting thing to happen around here was Shakespeare. Nothing notable since.

Perhaps it felt safe. Work the job. Buy the clothes. Finance the car. Pay the bills. Go to the pub. Eat the same dinner.

I couldn't do it. I couldn't live this day for the next 60 years, or longer and feel content. It might feel safe, but I felt like monotony was becoming deadlier by the second.

The trouble was, all our wages went on paying Dad's rent – every Friday a reminder text would ping through. 'Rent money.' Sometimes just 'rent'. Like we'd forget.

So short term, our escape was at Wilding Spa. A luxury health spa on the edge of town. It was our silver lining. We took great pride in being members there, although Ryan would park his battered old Renault Clio right up the other end of the car park, behind the shrubs. So no one would see us getting out of it and realise we didn't belong there.

Everyone knew of course. We stayed for lunch in the restaurant one Saturday afternoon, and asked to open a tab. We weren't sure what we wanted and figured it'd be easier to have whatever and then pay at the end. A proper treat. We'd saved our money so we could have our pick of the menu.

'I'm sorry, we don't do that here.' The manager sneered down at us.

'Payment will be required for each course.'

We didn't rise to it. 'Well, we were going to pay for it all at the end, like everyone else.' Ryan replied, as politely he could.

'It's our policy, sir.'

It wasn't and I knew it wasn't, but also I knew they thought less of us from the way I was followed round the spa treatments display. As though I'd pocket a bottle of expensive serum and dash out the door.

We paid the same as every other client there, but it didn't matter. We were skint. Everyone we know was also skint, they were just pretending not to be. Ryan and I took part in the charade, with our clothes, and hair and my make up. Our shoes, and bags and choices of drink. We played pretend just like everyone else, but because we knew we were faking it, it revealed everyone else to be a fake too.

The whole charade was pointless, but still, we continued doing it. Even the manager, who spent her shift looking down at us, was skint. If she wasn't, she'd have been enjoying the spa treatments next to us, not booking them in for us.

Still, she couldn't officially ban us from the premises, but she certainly made us feel unwelcome.

It seemed that even here, our sanctuary from outside – we still weren't free.

****

We returned to the Spa daily, ignoring the managers false smile when we entered the reception. Beaming at us for everyone else's benefit, before sliding into a grimace that we'd returned.

This afternoon was different. I'd just been called into a meeting at work, and told I was on my third, and final warning. This time it was for reclining in my chair during a phone call. I'd argued my case, as usual – we worked in a call centre, in-bound calls only. I'd advised the customer I needed a serial number to continue with the call and the customer had placed their phone down to find the elusive code. Being hunched over all day, I'd leant back to stretch, catching the eye of Jodie, our team leader, sixth in command of the office and someone who did not like me. At all.

I'd spent hours trying to figure out exactly what I had done to Jodie to warrant such an intense dislike, at first I'd tried to make up for whatever it was by being overly nice, but that seemed to make her hate me more. So, I'd taken a quieter approach, not drawing any attention to myself. Then Ryan had joined the team and Jodie had taken quite a liking to him on his first day. When he made a beeline for me during the break, Jodie's face had turned to thunder.

Then the real games began.

Jodie made it her mission to ensure I felt as isolated as possible. I had enough of that at home, so it was a familiar place to be. But that didn't make it any easier. At every opportunity she would create situations with private jokes that I wasn't a part of. She'd call meetings and 'forget' to let me know. Or schedule them during my breaks.

She created a seating plan, that had no changes, except Ryan's seat was to be on her line, and mine was the other end of the room. Alone.

 Jodie would often appear, lips pursed, sighing as she stood over me. I felt watched all the time, and as it was her job to monitor calls, I'd find that she would pick two calls at random from everyone else, but go through mine with a fine comb, hunting for a mistake to pull me up on. Had we been alone in the office, she'd have probably pulled my hair or yanked my chair out from under me. That sort of childish behaviour I'd prefer, so I could at least retaliate and punch her in the tits.

Instead she worked slyly. Pulling favours with the managers above her, so even if I had tried to explain that her treatment of me was unfair, they'd brush it off, and laugh about it during their daily lunchtime meetings with her.

The office was small, and the politics were vast. It seemed that everyone wanted to be a part of this tiny world, forgetting that a real world was just out of the glass doors. Popularity mattered, and thanks to Jodie, being seen talking to me wouldn't gain you any favours.

That afternoon, I had ended a phone call, and was called into a tiny office to face the Kangaroo court once again. This had happened several times over the last two months, meetings sprung on me at the last second. Each reason for such an 'official' meeting more bizarre than the last.

Jodie tutted once I had sat down. Another manager was there to take notes. I was feeling fiendish, so I pointed to his stack of paper.

'That's not allowed.' I told him, sagely.

A few weeks earlier, I had been caught doodling on a scrap piece of paper whilst waiting for a call. Lots of us it did it, to pass the time.

Jodie had seen me doing it, called a meeting, and the next morning - all paper in the office was banned. No questions asked.

Except there were questions, because this was a fucking office. And we needed paper, to, you know, function.

 We were told it was to do with data protection and to stop potential fraud, but as we were all zero-hour contract, minimum wage workers, not one of us gave a single shit about 'stealing' someone's email address or telephone number. We never dealt with bank accounts or anything like that. Just serial numbers, and a contact. Most of us wouldn't even know what to do with someone else's postal address, or phone number anyway, we needed our jobs too much.

Our managers explained the new protocol and then gathered any stray sheets of paper lurking around the office, Jodie had watched the paper ban come into play and smirked at me knowingly. A paperless office. The first of its kind surely. She'd won that round.

Within a few days stray paper had found its way back into the office, our computer systems were old and often crashed, meaning we'd have to take notes quickly before ending a call. I casually pointed out the necessity of paper, but Jodie's eyes narrowed, and she held fast.

Ryan pointed out that we all still had pens. If we wanted to steal details, we could just write them down on something else. Jodie scowled back.

I was handed a disciplinary notice for my bad attitude a few hours later, Jodie smug that she'd thought of a reason to penalise me. I made the notice into a paper aeroplane and flew it back over to her.

'But paper is not allowed!' I'd protested.

An hour later – fucking disciplinary.

Now, sat in the tiny office, Jodie was fuming at me again. She told me that it didn't matter that a customer wasn't physically on the phone while I lazed about, it didn't look professional.

'A customer could walk through that door and see you lounging around, and then what would they think?' She raved. 'Hmm?!'

'But customers aren't allowed to know where the office is based. Who's going to see me?' I asked.

It was a valid point, we were expressly told during training that no one could know the address, in case of bomb threats and things like that. We were also told that clients never came to see the office either. I didn't know why I was arguing back, it was a pointless exercise, one that only earned me more punishment. But I never wanted to go down without fighting.

'That doesn't matter!' Jodie's forehead was sporting a particularly angry vein. Her ice white hair was luminous against her pink skin. She wanted me out- but hadn't yet found a valid enough reason. And one doesn't want to get sued for unfair dismissal.

I knew my job was hanging by a thread, and that had nothing to do with my actual performance. I worked hard, and I knew I was good at my job. I decided against arguing back, and instead focussed my attention on The Vein.

'This is your third and final warning. I wouldn't find it so funny.' Her usually sickly-sweet voice that she put on for the other managers benefit was cracking. Her Pandora bracelet jingling on her wrist as she threw her hands up in despair at my insolent behaviour.

I stared at The Vein.

It wasn't fair. It wasn't fair that I was being treated this way, every single day. Not allowed to touch any paper to pass the time, Ryan and I were now even being forced to take opposite shifts, whilst everyone else had shifts with their work friends, family and partners. It wasn't fair, but then, of course - hadn't I learnt that by now?

Life is unfair.

After a thorough telling off and a reminder that I'd be receiving an official letter about my poor performance, and one last evil smirk from Jodie – I was permitted to go.

Just before I pushed through the doors to the car park, I caught sight of Jodie touching her head where The Vein was. She caught me looking and gave me a dirty look. Well, The Vein staring had probably just cost me my job. But damn it, it was worth it.

Ryan was sat in his car waiting – it was his day off today of course, punishment for being with me. He would have to waste a day off alone, and when it was my day off, I had to do the same.

Emotion rose up my throat painfully. God, they were so *frustrating*. It was so unfair, but I felt so stupid for feeling that way. It all sounded so pathetic. I couldn't let them get to me, but it was so *hard*. I knew there would be a letter waiting for me on the desk – open for anyone to read, a form of humiliation Jodie loved to orchestrate. It would detail, officially what I had done wrong, and how I must behave from then on. I was an adult, for fucks sake, but here I felt like a school child in detention.

I threw myself into Ryan's car.

'Ugh.'

Ahh, Ryan. My boyfriend, and my best friend.

Really- we had been best friends first, which seemed like such an underwhelming term for how I felt about him. I realised I was in love with Ryan when I hugged him close and it still didn't feel close enough. If I could I'd wear him, not like a psychopath, but like a furry blanket on a cold day. That close.

When I'd asked Ryan at what point he realised he had fallen in love with me, and he'd told me that he knew he was in deep; when I farted and he *'tried to smell it.'*

I stared at him now, as he began driving us away from the hell hole we worked in and marvelled once again at how brilliant he is. He smiled knowingly.

'Let's talk about it all in a minute, I've got your swimming stuff. Let's go relax.' He held up two towels, his grin getting wider.

It sounded like a fucking wonderful idea.

****

Once we were through those spa doors, past the old hag at the reception desk making no effort to hide her eye rolling that we'd turned up, again - nothing outside mattered. Just for a bit.

We sank into the jacuzzi, dipping underwater for a moment, as though washing off all the stress from our skin and rose again. Ryan made everything just melt away. He was how I imagined it felt to walk through the door of a beautiful house, knowing it's all yours, and you can shut the door on everything else – how home must feel.

I told him about the whole work saga. We mulled it over, a silent conversation bouncing between us at the same time.

Ryan turned to me, and asked 'If you could be anywhere, instead of here. Where would you go?'

I thought about it.

The coast swam into my mind.

Sun on our faces and sea stretching for miles, and no one else except him.

I answered honestly, but as dreamily as I did when he asked me what I'd spend the lottery money on if I won it.

'The beach...'

When I looked back at him, I realised it was different. This was a serious question.

'So, why don't we just go...?'

Ryan swam over and looked me in the eye. It was unnerving. He wasn't messing around.

I felt muddled up instantly. Dysfunction does that to you, it blurs the lines between reality and dreams and serious and jokes. Dysfunction means nothing is really for certain, and trips you up whenever you think you know the plan. Is this an adventure, or is it being ridiculous? I didn't know.

'Aren't we being a little melodramatic?' I broke his gaze, I wasn't really asking, I was just giving an escape route. A chance to laugh it off. A chance to remain on our current boring, soul crushing, systematic but 'safe' path.

'About what? What is really keeping us here?' He asked again.

The jets stopped whirring, the waterfalls stopped gushing and the whole room, with just us in it, plunged into a strange silence. The lights in the floor gave out an eerie glow.

Could we just walk away from it all? Leave our awful jobs, leave Dad's house, pack everything we could fit into Ryan's dodgy old Clio and just – drive away...?

The notion was tempting. Anything had to be better than this.

People talk about it all the time, don't they? Pack your problems up and start again something new. Somewhere different. A new life. I closed my eyes and tried to imagine something different. I couldn't. It was a pipe dream.

Ryan was challenging it now, and my head was full of conflict. Why does it have to be a whim? A fantasy? Why can't we just go for it? Then a quieter, almost a whisper in my brain...what was stopping me?

There was an electric, dangerous feeling in the air. Ryan noticed it too. It was that feeling you get when you spot a 'Keep Out' sign but carry on walking. Deeper into the dark woods, not sure what you'll find.

I wasn't happy here. That was the truth.

Every day here I was miserable. There was no time for living, only existing. I knew I was here for more than to just pay bills and die. There had to be more, but when were we ever going to find it?

Not working a dead-end job and living at Dads. That was for sure.

'We've got some money, we could do this…' Ryan wasn't trying to convince me, but I found myself nodding. We could do this. We should. It was now or never, surely. Perhaps having no reason to stay was enough reason to go?

There it was, a decision opening up in front of me. To step forward and agree would mean change. Growth. A new start.

To step back would mean safety. But stillness.

I was meant for more than this. As was Ryan. I couldn't explain it, I just *felt* it.

There was only one way to go. I nodded to Ryan, a smile growing on my face.

'Let's do it. Me and you. Let's go...'

'Me and you.' Ryan repeated. Like he liked the sound of it. Like it gave him purpose.

'Let's do this.'

******

Time seemed to speed up, as we dashed out of the jacuzzi and into our separate changing rooms. We were going. We were doing it. Life was happening right now; it wouldn't wait a second longer.

I'd grinned back at Ryan, cutting our invisibly tight strings to our life as it was and said it again.

'Let's go.'

So - we were going.

I got dressed quickly, my clothes sticking to my damp skin, hair flat to my head and soaking wet, but it was free! We were free! we hadn't even done anything yet, but it felt amazing!

An older woman came out of a cubicle and stared at me, looking at my wild smile and wet hair and sneering as she turned away. I don't belong here, she knows it. I know it. Well, fuck off, old lady. I'm free!

As I pushed through the double doors and collided with Ryan who had the same wild grin as I did, we held hands and ran out of the spa. The duty manager, who had held us in contempt the moment we'd stepped through the door as members of the 'club' that we didn't really belong in, she tutted as we sped past. Well, you can fuck off too, woman!

Had my spirits not been so euphoric, I'd have probably given her the double fingers as we flew past. But as of now,

I didn't care. I didn't care that she hated us being part of their club, I didn't care that the other members refused to acknowledge us. I just didn't care!

We threw open the glass door and jumped down the steps, 'See you never!' Ryan whooped on his way down.

Our high spirits travelled with us all the way back to Dads, right up until we reached the driveway.

As we pulled up, the house was in darkness.

I felt as though someone had poured cold water on the heat of our excitement. There was a storm brewing in there, I could sense it. I used to be able to tell if Dad was in one of his moods before I could even see the front door. And now it was like there was a very tangible black cloud cloaking the place. I pushed through the anxious feeling rising in my throat.

Not this time, I force the feeling back down. This time I was ready to tell Dad to go fuck himself.

I threw open the back door and jumped up the stairs, my mind in overdrive. I'd spotted Dad sat in the living room. The lights were off, the television was off. He did this in a calculated way. Normally – although I use that erm loosely… he would create a scene that would force you to pop your head in, and ask 'Everything alright?'

Then he'd attack. He'd have sat stewing on whatever minor offence had happened for hours. And I mean hours. Seething away until the moment he saw my face, or my brothers face, or whoever was unlucky enough to be the first to fall for the trap – then he'd let rip.

One time this happened when I had a bath. No one was in, I'd flicked the hot water on for an hour and enjoyed a glorious, rare bath. Bubbles poured over the sides, the books on the shelf curling in the heat. Then he and my brother walked through the door. There was no denying what I'd been up to, the steam and scent of every bath product I own was just too obvious. You could see it curling round the beams in the kitchen, pressing against the windows.

I'd emerged from the bathroom like a guilty puppy. Still wrapped in a towel. I knew I had to walk in and take my punishment like a man. A wo-man.

Dad had gone for it. He called me a selfish bitch and a whore. Accused me of all sorts of ridiculous things. I'd had enough. I pushed past him to go upstairs. I wasn't going to listen to this rubbish while I was still dripping wet. I might as well have the hairdryer on and drown the wanker out.

As I put my foot on the bottom step, he grabbed my arm so roughly I nearly lost my balance.

'Don't you walk away from me, you little bitch!'

He raised his hand and I thought he was going to slap me, so I got in there first and landed a series of punches to his head and face. 'Get off me!' I screeched, although it was me hitting him. It didn't feel real, just like a dream sequence. This scene had played out in so many other ways before, with my sister, my mum, even my brother. But I was hitting back, and hard. I'd wake up in a minute, and then decide against having the bath in the first place.

He grabbed my arm and wouldn't let go, and I only had one hand free, the other was holding up my towel. It all got messy from there, my brother wanting to defend both of us, his allegiance pulling himself in both directions... In the end, Dad threw me out of the house, still in my towel and locked the door.

Dad wasn't like this before, when I was a little kid. He'd been wonderful, and fun. He'd been my hero, my favourite person on the planet. I'd agonized over imaginary questions like 'Who do you love more – Mum or Dad?' He'd taught us all these interesting things about life, challenging our perspectives and encouraging us to have a mind of our own, he'd pushed us to become the individuals we are now. But somewhere along the way he'd changed. His bad moods became more frequent. His drinking too. Instead of wanting us to be the young adults we were, he spent his time trying to control what 'went on under his roof.'

I reminded myself of that incident as I sped up the stairs, into our bedroom and began throwing clothes into a bag. Ryan closely followed, looking like he wasn't sure if this was happening or not. It was.

It was.

 It was.

It was now or never. I grabbed our toothbrushes and threw those in. It is happening. I folded our pillows and duvet into a huge lump. It is happening.

Minutes later, we couldn't fit anything else into our bags. We'd chosen carefully. Clothes, some shoes and deodorant. We would come back for the rest.

We raced back down the stairs before Dad could catch us. I didn't look back. I didn't say goodbye.

Life wouldn't wait anymore.

Chapter 2 - The Lake

Music was playing softly, and the familiar motion of a car moving woke me. It was dark outside, and Ryan was swearing under his breath.

'Are we lost?' I asked, forgetting where we were, and what we were doing.

He patted my leg in reply. 'No. We've just passed Bodmin!'

Cornwall. The coast. We were here. Oh my god. We'd done it.

I sat upright to take in the surroundings but there wasn't much to see. Roads signs with places I didn't recognise swept past us. I checked the time.

2AM.

I thought back to the hours earlier, throwing our things into the car, driving away, out of Gloucestershire. We'd held hands wordlessly as we left our old lives behind, light and airy relief replaced feelings of heavy anxiety, hope replaced our fears. The invisible weight had lifted. As we passed the 'Welcome to Gloucestershire' sign, I cried with relief.

We'd stopped at a motorway service once we were out of the county and bought cheesecake to celebrate, Marks and Spencer's finest. Fuck the budget. We would worry about that later. We'd worry about it all later.

Then we chatted, sang and silently watched the world we knew fall away, ready to explore all the new possibilities ahead.

Driving around now we were here, we quickly realised we probably should have put some sort of plans in place. We'd been so caught up in the act of *going*, that we hadn't considered what to do when we'd *gone*.

Ryan had some family in Cornwall, his uncle and aunt that we'd stayed with a few months earlier at Christmas. And his Nanny and Grandad, who had taken the plunge and moved here a year earlier. Ryan considered staying at theirs for the night, but we couldn't turn up on their doorstep at this hour.

We spotted a few campsite signs and followed one up to a dark and empty looking site instead.

We figured we could park up and pay in the morning. No harm, no foul.

I pointed ahead to a small gateway; vision blurry now from having my contact lenses in for so long. We took the little track ahead, but the car started sliding down a hidden steep decline.

'Shit!'

The mist had settled on the grass and with no track to follow, the car slid down, down, down...

'Fucking Hell!' I breathed a sigh of relief, as the car glided to a stop at the bottom, squinting around but seeing nothing. No other caravans or cars were down here for whatever reason, so at least we hadn't been seen. Time to pull the duvet over us and get some rest, our new lives would begin tomorrow.

****

As the sun rose, the car began to heat up, forcing us to wake up and face the day ahead. Groggily, I rubbed my eyes and squinted around. In front of the car was a sign, I leaned forward to get a closer look, scrabbling for another pair of contact lenses as I did so.

I blinked and the sign a few feet away from the car came into focus.

DANGER

DEEP WATER

Shit. A few metres further and a huge lake spread out in front of us, if we had been going any faster, we would have slid straight in, car and all. I touched Ryan's arm to wake him properly. He had the same response as I to the immediate danger in front of us.

'Shit.'

We looked out the back window at the tyre tracks we'd left in our wake. The long grass was still soaked with dew, the tyre tracks careening from the top of the hill.

'If we were going any faster- '

'I know...'

'That was bloody lucky...'

'I know.'

'We'd better get going.'

I agreed. Time to get started, we had woken up in sunny Cornwall, albeit only just. Let's not waste a minute. Ryan got the car started and we began to drive back up the way we came, but the grass was still so wet that the tyres wouldn't stick to it. With no traction we began sliding back down the hill, and now we knew what lurked at the bottom. Well, let's say it wasn't a quiet journey back down.

Three attempts it took us to get out of that field, each one more terrifying than the last. Each time we knew the tyres were only getting wetter and the huge body of water was getting closer. But we made it, and we wasted no time getting straight out of there, it felt like if we stopped the car again it wouldn't get started, and we didn't want to get in any trouble for tearing up the field we'd left behind. So, we sped out of the gates and made our way to the beach, first stop – breakfast.

****

We found a café in Looe, and a spot by a window – conveniently with a plug socket in the wall to charge our phones. 'That's a homeless top tip,' I told Ryan. 'For the cost of just one cuppa we can charge our mobile. No home, no problem!'

We drank our tea and waited for our breakfast, people-watching as everyone went about their daily routines. People-watching is one of my favourite past times, and I don't think it will ever not fascinate me to think that every single person walking past, driving by, sitting next to us – each has a life that is just as unique as mine. They have their friends, and family, pets, favourite things. Even funnier to know that every person flitting by will do a turd that day.

It amused me to think that no one around us knew what we'd done. To anyone else we looked like a young couple, getting breakfast together before work. They had no idea that all our belongings were crammed into a car; parked just around the corner.

No one knew, but the grin on my face might have given it away.

Just then, my phone rang.

'Hell- '

'Gylisa, its Mike. Why aren't you in work?'

Ah fuck. Back to reality. What were we doing?!

I was supposed to be sat at my desk – I checked the time on the clock tower outside- 35 minutes ago. I was supposed to be there, but I was here, bunking off.

I ran over it all in my head, not believing it myself.

'...Well?!' Mike asked again, irate now. My vision focused. This was it.

'I won't be in today.' He could hear the smirk in my voice.

'And why is that?' He asked, knowing I had no good reason to not be in today, knowing he was about to tell me I had to turn up within the next hour or lose my job.

Well, I did have a good reason.

'I won't be in today-' I began, turning so Ryan could see me deliver my next line with a huge grin on my face. '-because I'm in Cornwall, about to have a slap-up breakfast, and then I'll be going to sunbathe on the beach.'

Mike was speechless.

Then I could hear a high-pitched screechy voice in the background. Jodie, who so often felt personally victimized by my existence, was about to get a shock. She began asking what I meant by that. Did I know I'd lose my job? Did I know I was on my last warning? What about Ryan? He'd lose his job too. She said it as though it would change my mind. As though there would be nothing worse in the world than to lose our incredibly sought-after crappy call centre jobs.

They were there, in a stuffy office, with no window and no air con. Their whole world revolving around their low-paid dead-end jobs. And I was here, in Cornwall. The sun was shining. The birds were singing. The possibilities were endless. So, we nearly drowned on our first night - And? What's life without a little adventure. And life in that office was life without adventure. It was life with timed piss breaks for God's sake. I didn't care what happened to me here, because whatever awaited us, it had to better than being there.

'Fuck your job.' I said. And hung up.

Later I found out from a friend in the office, as we did have a few, which irked the managers even more - that the shit had hit the fan once I hung up the call. Jodie was so angry, the veins in her temples came close to bursting and took it out on everyone. I felt bad about that for all of one second.

It wasn't my behaviour that made her do that, it was her own. There is no cause and effect, just an adult deciding that if they are miserable, everyone else should be too. As we ate our breakfasts, and meandered down to the beach, bellies full, ready for a proper nap, we'd left chaos in our wake.

And that, I thought, is my first real lesson, Dad.

'If you don't want people to screw you over, then you should treat them better when you have the chance.

Life isn't unfair, people are.'

Chapter 3 – Don't play the victim.

The days turned into weeks quicker than we could count them.

We watched sunsets and sunrises and stopped counting them after a while. Cornwall felt like our own utopia. A never-ending holiday. The right decision.

We sit with a coffee and a cup of tea on a café balcony, looking out at the sea below us. I turn and look towards the streets behind us and notice a dishevelled man rearranging carboard boxes in an empty shop doorway. Homeless. Nowhere to go. I watch him for a moment, a feeling I can't describe squeezes me momentarily. How did he get there, I wonder? What went wrong? People step around him. Seems I'm the only one to really 'see' him.

Ryan interrupts my thoughts, pushing a bowl of chips towards me.

'Have some before I finish the whole thing bab.'

I take one. When I turn back to watch the homeless man, he has moved on. I search the street for him, but he has disappeared into the shadows.

We dip in and out of shops, some with 'Job Vacancy' signs, which we ask about- but all of them requiring us to apply online and need us to have an address to apply from. We glaze over that bit, safe in the hope that we have some money to find a place to rent, if only enough for a month's rent. Maybe we could save up enough living like this for a deposit? I didn't know how mortgages worked, but I knew we couldn't save up that much money. How did everyone else do it? Did they get help? I didn't know. I did know, that my parents would never be able to help with a deposit, never mind Ryan's. Perhaps that was the only way. Some people got help, and some people didn't. I thought about my peers back home. Was it the norm to get money from your Mum and Dad? I couldn't relate.

We would have to try to private rent first, failing that, we can ask the council for some advice.

We feel safe in our decision. First one, done.

There's always a safety net, we tell ourselves. We've got loads of time to get settled.

I ring them one afternoon to ask about housing.

The guy on the phone asks me where we come from and I tell him.

'We are from the Midlands. Uh, but we left.' I gloss over the long-winded explanation. People must pull this card all the time. 'I just want some advice on, um, if you know how we could get somewhere to live.'

I word it wrong, but I don't realise that at the time. His tone switches from polite to irritated.

'You are intentionally homeless; we don't hold responsibility for you. Your home county might house you, but you'd have to go back there.'

'No, I know that. Well, I don't agree about being intentionally-, look. I just don't know what I'm doing and could do with some help.'

'Where are you staying tonight?'

'I don't know, we haven't- '

'There's more than you? Do you have a child?'

I look at Ryan who is frowning at me and picking at his finger.

 'No. Me and my boyfriend- '

'You could qualify for a hostel but not together I'm afraid.' He interrupts and sounds like he's rolling his eyes. I wonder if they have phone calls like this often. I feel naïve and uncomfortable. The conversation goes around in circles, I feel as though he is waiting for a certain combination of words before he grants me any guidance, but I don't know which the right ones are to say. Deflated, I end the call.

I don't want a free house; I want some advice on how to rent any house. But I haven't worded it correctly.

What is the point of a system that none of us are taught about, that is impossible to navigate without experience?

I brush off the phone call. Something will come up, I figure. It usually does.

We realise we are near Cawsand, which is where Ryan's relatives live. We stayed with them over Christmas a few months ago. Ryan sends them a text to see if they are around. 'It'll be expected' He says. 'If they see we are here and haven't said hello they'll think we are being rude.'

So, a text is sent, and one pings back…

'Come over, will stick the kettle on!'

A cup of tea, that always sorts everything out. That's exactly what we need.

****

We pull up outside and as I get out of the car, Ryan grabs my arm.

'Just a cup of tea, alright? Nothing else.'

His tone is off, warning me. About what though, I'm not sure. We've been here before, at Christmas and it was a great time. I love Ryan's family. But Ryan doesn't warn for no reason. And I trust him, so I nod in reply.

'Ok. Just a cup of tea.'

We are welcomed in with open arms, herded into the living room and plied with tea so we could tell them all about why we were here and what had happened. Ryan was still on guard, which I found strange, but I know families can be weird, so tell myself it's probably just a pride thing...

'That's a brilliant idea,' They beamed. 'You two will love life down here!'

That's what we hoped, we say. But we've got no idea where to begin...

'Well, where are you staying tonight?' They cut to the chase. Ryan's arm stiffens next to mine.

I look at him. This was what he meant. Just a cup of tea. Nothing else. I didn't see why; f=if it was just one night? The lure of a proper bed was tempting, but I trusted him.

'We were, uh, going to camp tonight. That's what we've been doing, so...'

'No way, absolutely not.' They wouldn't hear of it. 'At least stay here for a bit. We can help you with your job searches, finding a flat. We do know the area...'

I made a non-committal noise, hoping Ryan would be the rude one and say no. He tried, but not hard enough. It did sound promising, a hot shower in the morning. A warm bed. Even watching the TV appealed, and we hadn't watched television in months. Despite paying Dad so much rent, we weren't allowed to use the TV when he was in...which was all the fucking time.

We spend the evening watching Glastonbury highlights, and laughing together over glasses of wine. This is how home should feel, I think to myself.

I wonder what Dad is up to now, if he has any idea that we aren't coming home. Is he still sat there in the dark? Is he well?

Someone says something funny and laughter pierces my thoughts again. I might not know what the future holds, but for right now – this feels right.

Before we know it, the spare bedroom was set up and Ryan had brought our suitcase in. When the bedroom door shut Ryan hissed at me. 'What did I say before we came in? This is how it starts!'

'Me?! I didn't say yes!'

'You didn't say no either...'

'No, you did a great job of that!'

I point at our suitcase on the bed.

'One night. We will have showers, and then get going again.' He swore. I agree.

'One night.'

What was the worst that could happen? I reasoned once the lights were off, it'll be one night. One comfortable, welcome night.

That was two weeks ago.

• •

Every morning since we have to explain why we haven't found jobs overnight, and every time we try to leave to stay elsewhere and make our own way - they won't hear it that we don't have a proper roof over our heads. We escaped one night to camp near Newquay, under the guise of looking for work but finding jobs isn't not as easy as it was years ago.

Everything is online, we are told repeatedly.

The atmosphere feels awkward, and I can't bear it. Apartment listings are pushed under our nose over breakfast, huffing that we didn't look before they did. But they go out to get the paper, so they get to read it first.

Besides, they are all places we can't afford. Our bank balance is dangerously low now, I've looked.

We buy milk and bread when we go out in the day to 'pound the pavement looking for work', but as everything is online and we are redirected to website after website, we just use the time to be out of the house. I try to explain to that things are different nowadays, but they won't hear of it.

He thinks we are wasting time, and well, we are. But not how they think, it's all just so confusing and now we feel trapped here. I try and help out by keeping the place clean and tidy, and we go to the laundrette with our clothes. But then I feel like it's time I should be using online looking for job vacancies. If I sit down to use the computer, I feel as though I'm being lazy. We can't seem to win this one.

I have only been offered two jobs, both network marketing jobs which are useless at the best of times, but even more so now I'm 200 odd miles from my network. And even if I wanted to, I couldn't start because I don't have the initial outlay anyway. I suspect they are a scam, but of course, the man of the house disagrees and tells me so. He says anything is worth a try, anything is better than nothing. I don't agree, but I don't want to clash with him. I want them to like me, but it's hard when I feel so naïve about how to live with anyone else, what's normal and what isn't. So, I tend to keep quiet and out of the way.

I try to act grateful for their advice, even when it is unhelpful.

Ryan had a trial shift at a job, delivering fish. It sounded great, a proper Cornish job, down by the sea. But when he got back, he told us that he was expected to lease the van he'd be driving, pay for its services after so many miles, as well as buy all his stock at the start of each day. Anything left over wouldn't be refunded. As he knocked on door after door, he realised that it just wouldn't sell.

His family were not impressed.

The next morning, I sheepishly followed Ryan downstairs again and waited outside the bathroom while he took what can only be described as the longest piss in human history.

As I stood awkwardly by the door, I could hear loud whispering coming from the kitchen.

'You tell them now, but I've got to go to work...'

'You think I should just give it to them?'

'Yes, give it to them now and we can...'

They walk into the hallway, expressions I can't read on their faces.

'Morning!' I said breezily. I grinned with the optimism of a show choir. I opted against the jazz hands.

'I want you guys to read this...'

He pressed a piece of scrap paper into my hand.

'Oh-ok.'

Have you ever felt the light fall out of your body so quickly, you had to check your pants?

The familiar all-consuming creep of dread held my soul tighter than airport security. This was it. Something dreadful was about to happen. I waited for him to excuse himself into the living room before glancing down at the shaking paper in my hand.

The first line read 'Guys, you need to leave by...'

Oh god. Panic rose up in my throat. He was officially kicking us out, we hadn't even asked to stay in the first place! We'd tried to leave yesterday, again! But were told to stay, stay until things get sorted, stay until you have your flat. Stay while you work. And now this?

The grip of unfairness pinched me.

 Life's unfair, I get it Dad. It is.

Maybe Dad wasn't so harsh, maybe it was us. Two piss-taking idiots who don't know how life works.

And for the love of God is he STILL pissing?! I felt like kicking the door down, hurry *up* Ryan!

Just as I turned to let my foot meet the door, Ryan swung it open looking concerned.

We slipped upstairs to read the letters contents.

The letter said that we had two weeks before he wanted us to leave, that we had redirected our post to the house, that we used the internet too much, that we weren't looking for jobs hard enough. We hadn't offered to pay rent, and that we used too much water showering.

He then detailed that I'd left hair in the shower, and that he'd cleaned blood off the toilet which was disgusting. He'd underlined it.

As I read those words my face burned with shame. I had no idea. My thoughts started going at a million miles per hour. Who's blood? Did he think it was me? Was it me? What about the post – we'd been told to redirect the post for job offers. We'd been told to do all these things, but now they were being thrown back in our faces?

Ryan interjected.

'We only got our post sent there because he told us too! And the internet use was for job hunting mainly...we never intended to stay longer than a night and every time we'd offered money, when I had it, they said no?!'

He was venting, unable to understand the unfairness of it all. I didn't know what to say, too embarrassed to get past the part about blood on the toilet. Was it me? I didn't know. It had certainly never happened to me before. My face glowed red.

'I'm so embarrassed. I can't belie-'

'We are going.' Ryan interrupted. 'We can't stay here. I fucking knew it!'

He was speaking fast and firmly. This had all just been a stupid, silly mistake. Bloody adventure, my arse.

I began throwing my clothes back into the suitcase, straightening to room up. Sweating. Leave it like we'd never been here. Pretend this didn't happen. As we whizzed around the room trying to erase all evidence of our being here, they walked in.

'Look guys, you don't need to leave right now...it just needed saying that's all. Put your stuff down, we don't want to kick you out...'

I couldn't say anything, I couldn't even look at him. Shame, guilt and embarrassment seared my face, it filled my whole body with fire.

Ryan held his hand out.

'Look...' He shook their hands.

'Thankyou. Thank you for letting us stay so long. And for helping us with everything.'

He picked up our suitcase and made to leave, I quickly followed. I awkwardly paused by the door, unsure what to say.

I settle for, 'Yeah...thanks...'

For fucking nothing.

We swept out the house, Ryan throwing the suitcase in the car and turning on me.

'What did I fucking say when we got there the first night? What did I say?!'

I didn't know what to say, his anger was unsettling me. I felt like everyone was angry with me and this was all my fault. My fault for not fitting in at work, my fault for having a mad Dad. My fault for pushing us to leave it all and selling the dream. My fault for letting this all happen to us.

I burst into tears.

Ryan drove us up to a cliff top, and we sat in silence.

We'd really fucked it up.

Chapter 4 – The Lifeline

Ahh, the vastness of the sea.

As kids, we played a game on our way to our holiday cottage, whoever saw that wide blue line on the horizon first and announced, 'I can see the sea!', would win.

I'd be so taken in by its beauty every time it finally revealed itself to us, trundling along in the car, that I almost never won.

It never wears off. Not then. Not now.

I love looking at all the colours in that big blue *thing*. The enormity of it always makes me feel so small. Not small and pointless, but insignificant in a good way. It serves to put all my worries into perspective when I gaze to that line separating ocean from sky. It matters nothing to the sea whether I exist, whether I am worried. The waves will continue to come. The tides will carry on working.

Leaving in such a hurry seemed a bit bloody reckless now. We checked our banks to discover we had £23 left.

So we definitely couldn't afford a deposit now.

Shit.

The time had rolled around to 6pm. We'd had no lunch, our stomachs now making us very aware of that fact – although also adding to the ambience with their background whale noises.

Still, we felt stressed and…totally lost.

'What are we going to do?' Ryan asked, eyes wide and unblinking, still staring into the depths below.

I don't know. I really don't know. I usually know every time I'm in a sticky situation how to get out of it. I've seen violent fist fights in pubs. Ex boyfriend's drug driving veering out of control. Friends drinking their way into blood poisoning. Dad's thrown me out countless times, no money, no way to cry for help. And every time I've known what to do. How to survive. I always felt safe that I knew how to survive.

I've never been so broke I didn't know how to fix it.

But I don't know what to do right now.

When I was at college, I studied law. I was a natural at discovering loopholes and get-out clauses. I was an A* student. I was attentive and intelligent. I was set, my teacher told me, to become a brilliant solicitor. That combined with sheer luck, I never found myself in so much trouble I couldn't get out of it. But right now, I knew we were screwed.

We needed a miracle.

No sooner had I thought it, than Ryan's phone began to ring. Unknown number. He stared at it.

'Answer it.'

Ryan answered, and our miracle happened.

Like I said, I can find loopholes and escape routes. But sometimes all I've got is a bit of luck.

A guy on the other end wanted to offer an interview for a delivery driver job. Nervous thanks to the 'Fish Man with a Difference' job but knowing we had no choice, we said we'd be there, and off we set – destination: Plymouth.

****

With no money to stay anywhere else, we parked up somewhere inconspicuous and slept in the car. For the second time.

In the morning Ryan straightened himself out as much as he could for the impending interview. Although we both knew what hung on this opportunity, I didn't want the pressure to get too much for him.

'Don't worry, it's a good sign people are ringing us. Just try your best.'

He was gone for ages. I spent the time watching lorries go into the business estate where the depot was located. I people watched a little bit, but it wasn't anywhere near as interesting as the centre of town in Looe. I was struck by the realisation that that was only a few weeks ago and yet it felt like months and months. The false start of our new life.

I folded and refolded our clothes in the boot, wet wiped all the dashboard and sides and tidied everything up. I wanted everything to look nice for Ryan's return but only had the dusty car and some wet wipes to work with. Still, it looked alright. I was rolling the proverbial turd in glitter.

When Ryan got back, he told me all about it.

'It's just shoving boxes around.'

But on the second day he was offered a job as a proper delivery driver.

'A promotion already!' I'd praised.

The hours were 7am until 7pm, weekdays. For £7 an hour.

'Sevens my lucky number!' It seemed logic and reasoning had gone out the window. We were spiritualists now; it was all we had left.

However, it was a month in hand. So, we'd waiting a while to see any money. I thought about the flat we'd viewed a few weeks back, the first few days at Val's house.

 4 Tremar Apartments.

I kept imagining us living there. Would it still be empty in a months' time? I hoped so.

We drove down to a Tesco we'd spotted on the drive up, and decided we would have to make our £23, plus whatever change we had lurking in the car last. For a month. That's all.

'We can do it' Ryan told me. 'It's just four weeks.'

In Tesco, we wandered around for ages, I wanted to have a look at the home section and imagine decorating '4 Tremar Apartments'.

I did that a lot over the next few weeks, when they changed the furnishings around it would be so exciting. Then I began calculating how much it would all cost. It passed the time.

We decided the cheapest but most filling food, that was almost non-perishable would be – soup.

So, we bought tins and tins of the stuff.

Then we treated ourselves to a loaf of bread, telling ourselves we would ration out a slice per day. And then two bottles of 2litre water, at 19p per bottle. It became our routine food shop every few days – when the water ran out.

One week I went wild and bought some butter and plastic cutlery. I was certain Dad had told me butter doesn't go off. Turns out in 20-degree heat inside a car – it does. And fast.

The heat would get up so high in the car some days, I was forced to sit next to it, under the shade of a tree. It wasn't really a proper tree, more of a stick. But it was all the shelter I had. I did hang up some towels in the window to stop the sun beating down on the windows, but it was still a sweat box in there. And sweat – plus no budget for deodorant, does not maketh a pleasant pong.

I was quite innovative though, the soup straight out the tin was rank. At least I thought so – Ryan would manage to wolf it down regardless, but the poor sod was working 12 hours a day and watching the other lads clutter their vans with Burger King wrappers and other such junk. I might have been bored out of my mind with soup tins serving as my 'Wilson', but at least I couldn't see what I was missing out on.

Anyway, as it was getting so hot in the car, I'd lay out the two tins we'd have for supper to heat up in the window all day. By 5pm they'd be warm, and by 7.15pm – Ryan's home time, they'd still be warm enough to…enjoy.

It was funny really, how quickly we adapted and how we didn't even question what was happening to us. It still didn't feel real, I guess. Survival just kicked in. We'd quickly gone from holiday mode, to crisis mode, without so much as speaking about it. No one we knew lived around here, so it wasn't something we had to defend or explain.

Ryan had mentioned to his boss that he was living in his car, once he'd decided he was trustworthy enough. And his boss had told him it wasn't a problem, but it would have to end quickly – a business just doesn't want a homeless person working for them.

Ryan had promised by the end of the month, we'd have an address. His boss then said, once we did, Ryan would be allowed to use the work van to get to and from work.

We still didn't feel homeless. We reasoned so often that it was just a month, we'd count down the days and tell each other how we'd be laughing about this bit soon. It would be a blip in our life. A strange memory. We were just doing what we had to do to get by.

I'd think back to working in our old office, and it pained me to know that if our old managers could see what we were up to they'd be laughing at us. Telling themselves they knew we wouldn't be better off leaving.

But no matter how bored, or dirty or lonely I felt. It still wasn't as bad as getting up and going to that fucking job every day. It hurt my soul every day I clocked on, knowing I couldn't clock in a minute early, but I was forced to be there 15 minutes before a shift. And knowing that clocking out late was forbidden, even if a call ran past your leaving time.

So, I might be here, sweating in a car and eating soup straight from the can. But at least I'm free from those arseholes.

Chapter 5 – The Novelty of Survival.

A week had passed us by, and our strange situation still felt surreal; like we were having a little 'poverty taster trip'.

Every morning Ryan drove the car from an area we'd claimed as our sleeping space, to the business estate a mile or so away. The noise from the radio woke me, where Ryan's alarm did not. We'd been charging his phone at a plug socket we'd found unmanned near the toilets. We'd bootleg electric from there, wait until he was 'out the red' and then continue 'shopping'.

Ryan would head to work with no breakfast, but two tins of soup; his water and whatever else we may have found the money for the evening before. We had begun to run out of loose change in the car, but every now and then five pence would turn up, and we'd search again with fresh vigour.

I've always been quite lucky at finding random coins on the ground, so could generally rustle up 30p by 6pm, If I walked around for long enough. All the while, eyes glued to the pavement – like it was an entirely normal way to pass the time.

I think I have always found myself dissociating from surreal events. Never one to panic, you'll never find me screaming at the roadside of a crash or unsure what to do in an emergency. I just retreat into my mind and deal with it. One foot in front of the other. One day, hour or minute at a time.

Dad had his first diabetic hypo with my brother and I, home alone one day, we must have been about 7 years old. He had started acting a bit weird, which must have been very weird considering his usual state was bizarre in itself. We'd been huddled around the computer and he began lifting Tom up, too high, too dangerously. Tom had scraped his back on the broken chair arm, and I noticed Dads eyes had glazed over, as though he wasn't in there.

It was then that a memory of Mum telling me 'if your Dad starts acting funny, just get him a Twix or something' swam to the fore front of my mind.

It had seemed an odd thing to say at the time, but watching Dad throw my brother about the room giggling like a child had flung it forward in my brain. 'Tom,' I'd said calmly. 'Come here.'

My brother, glad for the interruption, scampered out of Dads reach and we shut him in the spare room. I explained what I thought was going on and he had the same suspicions. Now we had the trouble of getting him to eat a

Twix, which ended up being crushed and slung at the wall. We tried a warm tea, with a fuck load of sugars in, but that ended up on the floor too. It was like attempting to feed a very large, violent toddler. To an outsider, it would have been a shocking scene, two young children trying to feed their bear-like father, our protector, in such a way. But to us, well – it was just survival. A novelty.

Eventually we managed to get a syrup sandwich in him, although I worried briefly about him choking, I figured we were at a crossroads where either decision would end in death – so I could always step in and catapult a milky tea at him to help.

An hour and a half after the sandwich had been eaten, Dad was back to normal and didn't seem to recall any of what had happened.

We shrugged it off and continued with what we'd been doing. Mum got back not long after, and it became just another one of those things that none of us would mention. It was dealt with. That was that.

****

I wondered how Ryan got through the day, because sat in the car hour after hour felt like an alternative to Hell. Dad lent me a book once about all the different theories of Life After Death.

One of my favourite ideas of Hell was that all the time we spend doing things in life, we are sentenced to do in one continuous loop. For example, say that the average adult spends two weeks of their life sat at traffic lights. So, after Death, we will sit there in Limbo, for two weeks, at traffic lights. The average woman spends 1 year, 7 months and 15 days in the bathroom, and so on. Even things that seem pleasurable would be hellish if we had to do them for so long – an orgasm that lasts 5 months, or if you were particularly unlucky in life – a couple of minutes. Eating solidly for almost half of your life. Redoing every poo, you ever did in your lifetime, one after the other. Quite literally laying a cable. It fascinated me.

And here I was, in my waking life, living out that Hell.

Waiting. Waiting. Waiting.

When Ryan returned, I would be overjoyed!

It gave me a lot of sympathy for dogs left home alone all day while their owners worked – Ryan was back! If I had a tail, it would beat out a drum solo when I spotted Ryan returning to me.

However, Ryan would be so exhausted from work he'd throw himself in the car and we'd just hug it out for five minutes, not saying a word.

I felt for him every time it happened. He told me that the other lads would spend £10 a day or more on lunch, laughing at his lowly tins of soup. Sometimes they'd grab him a hotdog, but then he'd feel guilty about me back at the car.

Most of them didn't take the job seriously, they earnt more than him as their rounds were quicker, and as they were paid by parcel it worked out for them. They smoked in the vans and filled them with rubbish. If Ryan had to swap vans with someone he'd come back to his looking like a tip. Then he'd spend half an hour cleaning it out before heading back to the car, knowing it would probably happen all over again tomorrow.

'It's just for another couple of weeks' I'd promise him.

Tesco became our Wilding Spa. We'd swipe up any taster food if it was on offer. Wash in the sinks. And calculate what money we had to work with – whether we'd stretch the budget to fit in some bread.

It amazed me that we'd ever spent so much on food a month or so earlier, £85 on an evening meal that we wouldn't even finish. Now, counting change carefully to get the most basic of essentials. To go from one life to the other in a few weeks was polarizing. Was this poverty? I wasn't sure.

We weren't homeless people, oh no. We weren't like them. We were different. We didn't have the shabby clothes, or the cardboard box and newspaper bedding. We were just having a stop gap. That's all. It'll be all over in a week or two.

Wouldn't it?

We parked up near Tesco in the night, waiting for the cover of darkness to finally give us some privacy. We made makeshift curtains with some towels to keep out the streetlights but using them in the day just made us stick out more. The more under the radar we were – the better.

We soon found ourselves thrown into the spotlight anyway, but until then – we felt relatively safe, tucked away from the main streets, out of sight. Out of mind.

Every day we would have our 17p, 2litre bottles of water. I was worried about drinking enough because it was so hot now – midsummer. We might have been down on our luck in the housing stakes, but we still had our health and the last thing I wanted was for either of us to get sick, dehydrated or worse.

The trouble was, drinking two litres of water all day in the heat makes for one full bladder. And in the day, we were in the business estate. And I didn't *dream* of attempting to go into an office block or garage or whatever else to use the loo, plus I knew they'd get sick of it if I asked all the time. *'Under the radar'* Ryan would remind me.

So, I had to hold it and hold it until I felt like my bladder was going to rupture and then I'd force the last of the water down, and cut the bottle into two. I handily had packed a pencil case – it was useful for boredom, and the safety scissors it held.

With no privacy, there was very little in the way of shrubs, and the only fences were all chain link ones. I had begun to get paranoid about leaving the car unoccupied – it looked like it had been abandoned, a dated car, full of our stuff. I'd make a quick towel den, hiding the outside world momentarily, piss into one half of the bottle and hope it didn't overflow. Then I'd throw the wee under the car when there was no traffic around. It didn't make for a pleasant smell, but I figured – once the rain finally came it would all wash away.

And anyway, no one need know about it. We were under the radar.

Chapter 6 – The Security Guard

'Excuse me, miss?'

I flew forward, scared out of my skin. I'd had my eyes closed and had been daydreaming in lieu of watching television. For a moment I just stared at the guy interrupting the peace and assaulting my eyes with his bright hi-vis jacket.

'Hello?' He said it quieter this time, probably worried that he'd startled me.

I wound down the window a crack.

'A few people in the office have seen you here in the mornings, I just wanted to check you were alright?'

Shit. People had seen me. It wasn't such a surprise to hear that, but it was obvious from his gentle tone that they'd made their own assumptions and enough of them had mentioned it to this fella. My mind battled out the uncomfortable feeling that people had not only noticed me but thought it strange enough behaviour to comment on. It made it too real, it made it a problem. I didn't want to open that can of worms, not yet.

'I'm fine' I lied.

'Are you sure?'

'Yeah, honestly.'

He took his moment, now he was close enough to the car to peer in, to see our now rather dirty duvet, the tins in the window and clothes and towels chucked in the back. I hadn't had my afternoon spruce up yet, and I liked to save all the mess, so it kept me busy for at least 15 minutes. Now he was looking at it I wanted to throw myself over it, to save the humiliation. Too late.

'Ok.' Pursed his lips as though I'd really pled my case for things being fine, and well – there was just nothing else he could do. 'You just be careful.'

I made a face at his back as he left to head back inside the building nearby.

Fuck. I wished I could move the car now. Obviously, I couldn't even if I could drive – because Ryan wouldn't be able to find me.

Embarrassment washed over me. It felt like leaving Val's all over again. The shame of it. I was disgusting, I looked disgusting and people were noticing. I was so disgusting people were talking about it. Oh God.

Had they seen me weeing? Had they seen me eating soup from the tin?

How naïve we'd been to assume we were going under the radar. We were the most non-business-like characters in a fucking business park! Of course, our arrival would have been noticed – if it was my workplace, I would have noticed the minute a car pulled up with all this stuff in it. They mustn't ever see Ryan; he was gone long before rush hour began - so it would have looked like I was alone.

I suddenly felt very vulnerable.

****

When Ryan came back that evening, I'd hurriedly described everything that had happened, and he looked just as worried as I felt.

'That was a warning'.

I hadn't thought about it like that.

Now Ryan said it, it had seemed like that. I'd spent so long without any conversation that I hadn't picked up on it, plus I'd been so embarrassed by the state of the car I hadn't been thinking straight.

He hadn't been checking in. He'd been letting me know that I was becoming a nuisance. It was a subtle hint to 'move on.'

Just in case, we decided to keep to the same story if anyone else spoke to me, I'd simply say 'This is just temporary, I'll be gone at the end of the month, I am ok. We don't mean any trouble.'

The last thing we needed was the police to turn up, or for any more attention brought to us. We would be out of their way soon enough.

Only a few days later, I noticed an older guy in the same hi-vis making his way over to the car. Feeling a bit more prepared this time, the car was relatively tidy, and I smiled brightly at him, winding my window down all the way.

'Excuse me...' he began.

'Hi!' I beamed back. 'Are you ok?' I was overdoing it on the politeness, but I wanted him to bugger off quickly before any uncomfortable questions were asked. I was ready. Just tell them its temporary, and we don't mean any harm. We'll be gone soon. Iy'll be fine.

'Yeah. I just want you to know that you are being watched.'

His words felt like they winded me. Panic began to rise up.

'What?'

I cast my mind back to the compass I knew was in my pencil case, but it was under all sorts of stuff before I'd be able to get to it. It was the only thing I could think to use as a weapon, just in case. Oh Lord, I've been homeless for two weeks and I'm ready to shank a man. How things have changed. He sneered at me.

'You've been here for over two weeks. I know, I've seen ya. And you are being watched.'

He said each word so cruelly, that I didn't know how to reply.

'You've got no tax on your car, no MOT! It's not on!' As he carried on, he was getting more and more aggressive, spit was actually flying out of his mouth. '-We've paid our way, it's people like you who make it harder for the rest of us… and you…. you're breaking the law!'

Now I am used to taking shit from people. I had spent my whole life picking my battles with my Dad. I'd spent two years quietly accepting every insult that had come from my ex-boyfriends' mouth, and his friends laughing at my house or my clothes or my personality. And now this guy, a stranger…. knows nothing about me except what he'd seen for the last couple of weeks, which by anyone's standards, whether I wanted to admit it or not – was clearly a pretty dire situation to be in.

I knew about the tax on the car, I knew. I was the one who had frisbeed the expired disc out the window the day it ran out. I knew we didn't have the money to get another, and we didn't have internet access either. I knew. But there wasn't a fat lot I could do about it right now. It would all have to wait.

'I could ring the police right now you know, and they'll crush your car!' He said it so smugly, so pleased with himself. So full of glee that he had something over someone. It's funny what a little bit of power will do.

I'd seen it in Dad when he'd decide if the cat was going to get fed at 5pm, or 4pm. I'd seen it in him when he'd chosen whether I'd be allowed a bath that day, or …probably not. It was the twinkle that shone ever so slightly when they exercised their power over you.

I must have looked horrified in that moment; I've never been able to keep a poker face. 'I can read you like a book' everyone says to me.

The thought of everything we owned being taken away from us was already a very real fear. We worried about it every time the car trundled into our safe space in the evening, and back to the business estate every day. Everything we owned in the world was in the car, and we had nowhere else to put it all. My jewellery box with pieces that weren't worth anything in money but were priceless in sentiment. My clothes – each item quickly chosen to come with us, even things I'd never wear while we were living like this but had been too special to leave behind. Even our grubby old duvet and pillows, they were ours. They were our comfort.

This was all we had.

My head swam with emotions, and as I swallowed down my tears, I saw the guy stood in front of me, face smug watching my turmoil and my fear turned to fury.

This arsehole didn't know what I'd left behind. He didn't know why we'd ended up here. He didn't know how it felt to be cooped up in a smelly old car day in day out. All he knew was that I was living it, and obviously not paying any bills. His house and car and everything else were costing him, and instead of projecting his fury at the people that made that happen, he was turning it on me, someone who clearly had nothing, and was living life 'for free'. As far as he was concerned, he was 'picking up our bill.'

I looked him straight in the eye.

'How about you keep your fucking old nose out of my business?!'

He gasped at me. Shocked by the change of tone. This guy was the sort who liked women to stay quiet and unassuming. Well, that – I am not.

I punched the lock down, locking me inside the car. The old codger probably thought it was to keep me safe from him, but I could feel the red mist setting in, and how very satisfying it would be to stamp this guy's head into the kerb. I fancied my chances.

'You are disgusting' he spat at me, stamping off back to the building.

'So are you!' I shouted after him, somewhat lamely.

Immediately I felt sick. Really sick. He was probably in there right now calling the police, and it was going to be hours until Ryan was finished. If they turned up and took everything away, I couldn't just sit here, that security guard will be out moving me on.

I knew I'd handled it all wrong, I should have been polite. I should have just taken it.

I sat and I waited feeling like I was dying a thousand deaths waiting for the inevitable to happen. Any minute now the police would turn up, and that would be it. Game over.

I tidied the car. It was a pointless exercise seeing as it would be crushed in a few moments anyway, but it kept me busy.

'You're being watched' he'd said. And now I felt like there were hundreds of eyes on my back, just waiting for something as exciting as the police arriving.

I was so lost in my thoughts about it all that I didn't notice a white van pull up directly behind the car.

Chapter 7 – The Note

A horn honked, and I braced myself, ready for whatever fuckery was about to occur. And I was certain it would be something awful. Ahh well, it'll pass some time at least. I opened my eyes to peer behind me, who was that in there?

I turned around fully, to see Ryan waving madly in the drives seat of the van.

Oh my god! He wasn't waving, he was gesturing for me to –

'GET IN!' He called.

Well, I didn't need asking twice. I quickly grabbed my bottle of water and a cardigan and jumped into the van.

'Hello honey!' Ryan smiled. 'You're coming with me today!'

He was so excited at the prospect that it was hard not to join in, forget the security tosser, although I did tell Ryan about him as we sped along. But Ryan's jovial mood remained unbroken.

'Well, what can we do?' I'd said to him.

'Exactly, fuck all.' He shrugged. 'Better move the car though.'

We cruised along all day in that van, it didn't feel like work at all, except for the occasional interruption of conversation so Ryan could dropkick a parcel towards its destination. Just kidding, he carefully dropped each item off at its new home, and we were waved off by each customer. Some of them offered a drink, or cake. We accepted gladly!

We drove all around tiny villages that we'd never have discovered otherwise. Cornwall was vast, but quaint. Mad, but normal. The coastline appearing suddenly as we went around a bend never failed to take my breath away, but then – neither did the countryside.

I remembered why we'd been pulled there, as we drove along. This felt right, even though everything felt wrong right now. This was where it would happen. Everything would fall into place, never mind security men or police calls or anything else.

If we endured, we would be rewarded with a life to be proud of. I knew it.

As the day ended, the sun casting long shadows and painting the scenery bright orange, Ryan made a detour to drop me near the car.

'You're not really meant to be in here with me,' He told me. 'I could lose my job if we get caught.'

Ryan! I was shocked, if he'd have told me that I wouldn't have got in!

We needed this job. It was our last lifeline.

But as I walked back to the car, I realised we did need this job, but I think Ryan needed the company a lot more. The thought warmed me, as the sun finally slipped behind the buildings and a cold breeze passed through.

I reached the car and went to grab the handle, when something caught my eye.

A scrap of paper on the driver's seat.

Opening the door, I leaned in to pick it up. It was a small note.

In neat handwriting, written on this tiny piece of paper were the words:

Hi.

I've seen you sleeping in the car these last few weeks. I just thought if you needed anything...

My Number – 07506151743

Matt x

FUCK.

I got out the car, quickly checking all the doors and windows. I'd locked them, I was sure of it. The windows were all still closed, except for the sunroof. It had been open a tiny crack, but surely not enough to slide the note in? And it had been facing up on the chair. It looked like it had been placed there. But now I wasn't sure. I hadn't stopped to treat it like a crime scene, I'd just picked it up, my nosy side taking over. I'd make a rubbish copper.

I turned the note over in my fingers, looking for another clue, anything to show me where this had come from.

The security guards' words echoed in my mind again.

You are being watched.

I sat back in the car, locking the doors again. I couldn't stop myself looking around, checking in all the windows nearby for a face looking back at me. Cars began to drive past, and I realised it was home time.

Did one of these cars have 'Matt' in?

I looked back at the note. The neat, precise handwriting made me think Matt was quiet, perhaps a bit of neat freak. Just then, a car beeped as it drove by, my head jerking up to see, but I couldn't make out who was driving.

Was that Matt?

Was that him? Did he see I had gotten the note? Had he meant to speak to me, but I wasn't here?

Or was it the security guy giving me a final warning as he left to go to his home.

Perhaps it was someone else, a well-wisher maybe? Or someone taking the piss. That felt more likely. It was humiliating being here like a sitting duck. I realised we hadn't gone unnoticed at all; we were probably the talk of all the offices around us.

How had we swapped working in the office, to living outside of one. Like this.

I looked at the note again.

'Matt x'

What was I going to tell Ryan? Should I tell him? I wasn't sure, I suddenly felt like he'd be annoyed, jealous even, although I wasn't sure why. Half of me wanted to hide it. But the other felt guilty- I'd have to tell him.

But then what.

Should I text him? To let him know I'm fine? Or would that invite more attention.

What if he was a serial killer and he was testing the water to see if I'd be noticed if I disappeared. A shiver ran down my spine.

Ryan got back, and I showed him the note.

He frowned.

'Someone's been watching you then.' He seemed unnerved by it.

So, did I when he put it like that.

We would have to move the car.

Chapter 8 – The Police

As more days passed, we were yet to find somewhere truly safe to park the car, which was a downside of not knowing the area well. During rush hour I found myself shrinking back into the chair, hiding under the duvet – doing my best not to draw attention to myself. Pretending I wasn't there.

This wasn't permanent I would tell myself, over and over. It's just until the end of the month…

If someone walked by on the pavement, I'd sit stock still, or busy myself so they couldn't make eye contact. The feeling of judgement was unbearable. On worse days I used our two towels to block up the windows altogether, my only form of privacy against the world outside.

It was unbearably hot most days in the car, from lunchtime onwards. I'd open the doors a crack to let the breeze in, but some days there wasn't even that and I'd have to sit in the sweatbox and ration out my water wisely. It was on one of those hot days that I laid back against the headrest trying to coax myself into relaxing – when the phone rang.

It came as such a shock, no one had called the phone for so long that I had begun to assume that the thing didn't work. Texts came through from Orange, reminding me that we hadn't paid our phone bill, and then that we were being charged for not paying our phone bill, and then that our direct debit had been cancelled. And then that we were being charged on top for that. The bill was becoming unmanageable, but we didn't have the money to give, so every warning and threat of action had been ignored while the debt spiralled. Even when we got back on our feet, we'd be doing it with a handicap. It felt as though we were being punished for being poor.

 Anyway, they'd cut us off completely, so we couldn't ring them even if we wanted.

It was an unknown number calling, which immediately set me on edge. I've never received a call from someone using an unknown number that has turned out to be positive, let's put it that way. But curiosity got the better of me, and besides – it would give me something to do.

'Hello?'

'Is this Ryan?'

'No, I am his girlfriend though...'

'Gylissa?'

Shock pulsed through me. Who was this? How would they know my name?

'This is PC Alex-'

'Ok...'

'We've had reports that you have been sleeping in a car?'

Oh, for fucks sake.

'Y-Yeah...'

'Do you have a child with you?'

'What? No?!'

'Well, we have had reports of a child in a car on the estate...'

'Oh, no, we've got no kids. It's just us two. Just me in the day.'

'Right. And is it your car?'

'Yes. Well. It's Ryan's.'

'Can I speak to Ryan please?'

'No, sorry – it's just me here in the day. He's working.' Annoyance pulsed through me, she didn't get it wrong by mistake, she was trying to trip me up. She thought I was lying.

'Right. And do you know the car isn't taxed? Or insured?'

Bugger. I did know. But I didn't want to get into trouble for knowing. Should I play dumb? Would it get Ryan into trouble if I say anything? I didn't know the consequences of that. I didn't want to be a catalyst to it. So, I lied.

'No, I didn't know.'

I hate lying. I'm rubbish at it. Worse when its face to face. My best friend, Hannah, used to get me to lie to my parents about what we were up to. Whether it was the classic 'She's staying at mine, and I'm staying at hers' So we could bum about the village late at night, no one any the wiser. Well, until we got caught by my neighbour scaling her fence, her flashlight shining through the window casting a spotlight onto our dodgy doings.

One evening Hannah's mum had found cigarettes in her coat pocket, and Hannah had lied her way out of it. That was until her mum cornered me to ask me what I knew about them. I knew that Hannah was going to be found out anyway, and I didn't want to seem like I had form for lying. That may sound like an honourable way of thinking, but it was just in case we needed to lie our way out of something much more serious later.

As Hannah's mum held up the packet of cigarettes and Hannah stood behind her shaking her head and motioning 'no' with a hand at her neck. I caved and admitted they were hers. Hannah got a bollocking, but it did mean she didn't have to hide her smoking habit anymore, and when we got in trouble for something else later down the line – my word was gospel.

The memory of it set off a pang of homesickness. I missed Hannah. Had she not even noticed I'd gone?

'There's stuff hanging off it.' The Policewoman interrupted, sounding exasperated. Fury bubbled in me once more; I was starting to get sick of people butting in. 'You shouldn't be driving it.'

I felt like I was annoying her just by talking, her sarcastic tone, the way she was speaking to me as though I had an IQ of 2.

'I'm not driving it. If I was there wouldn't have been a report of us staying it in would there? We haven't moved it for ages.'

Her tone turned cold and biting immediately.

'You do know that if, and when you are caught driving it, it will be taken from you – don't you?'

I took a deep breath and exhaled. Of course, I know that, that is why we haven't moved it! What does she think we doing? A fucking experiment? What does she expect us to do? Drive it? Not drive it?

She must have taken my inhale of a deep breath as a sound of crying, because her tone shifted slightly. I was actually taking a moment to think about it before 'telling a police officer to Fuck Off' was added to my criminal record.

She must have heard me sighing, as her voice shifted slightly, and she spoke in a gentler tone.

'You are obviously sleeping in it for a reason, I just don't want you to lose everything...'

Finally, I felt like a human talking to another human again.

'Yes officer. Me either. Everything we have is in here,'

'Look, I'd prefer it if you could move it off the road. If something hit you, with no insurance...'

She trailed off.

'We will move it later today, when Ryan is back, I promise...'

She seemed pleased by that answer. 'Are you ok?'

'Yes, I'm fine.'

It didn't sound as though she was asking because it was her job now, but I didn't know where to begin. No one ever seems to teach us how to ask for help, I guess.

'Ok. Well move the car and I hope you find something more suitable soon. You can't stay there forever.'

I wondered if she was taught to treat anyone falling under the 'obviously without a roof over their head' category with a bit of 'tough love'. I know that most of my peers' attitudes were that homeless folk were druggies or 'ne'er-do-wells'.

I often felt that we are desensitised to other people's plight, as though anyone in circumstances worse off to our own – well they deserved it. Not sure how, but they did. It seemed to take a lot of empathy to understand that everyone else's journey doesn't follow the same route as our own.

'It's not forever. Just 'til the end of the month.'

'Make sure it is.'

With that, she rung off. I sighed with frustration.

Obviously that arsehole security guard had phoned the police, as he said he would. We had no choice now; we weren't welcome on any stretch of road near this business estate. It didn't matter how 'out the way' we were. We weren't wanted. Well, we didn't want to be here either, we were just trying to get by.

My frustration swirled into worry. What if someone was waiting for us to move and planned to phone the police the moment our car was on the road. The security man who had spoken to me had seemed the sort. It would make his day watching us get pulled over and left on the pavement with nothing but our dirty old duvet and some bags of clothes.

The image in my head, instead of filling me with fear made my mouth turn up instead. We'd be royally screwed, and then what?! Well, we'd have to set up camp on the pavement. Be Pavement-People. And I'd do it right outside that arsehole's door. I'd make myself his problem then! He'd rue the day he fucked it all up for us. Might even follow him home, set up camp there too.

I chuckled at the thought, anything than poke the creeping fear that we were dangerously close to losing it all. We were very much ON the radar now, and it wasn't a comfortable thought.

When you are staring up Shit Creek and find your hand without a paddle, well that's all you can do, I guess! As I pulled down the sun visor to look at myself smiling, I saw someone ambling towards the car in the reflection.

Oh, what fresh hell is this? Can't I get some bloody peace?!

As the guy got closer, I realised he was about the same age as me, a feeling of humiliation sank into my stomach and sat there. People like me should be in work, getting to grips with adulthood, not sat in a car, not doing anything. I'm just existing.

'Hi?' He seemed nervous to speak to me. 'Are you ok?'

'Hello?'

'I've been meaning to catch you, there's just – 'he puffed out '– There's a grumpy guy in there' He pointed back across his shoulder to a building nearby. 'He'd called the police, I thought ... I just thought you should know...'

'Yeah, thank you. I do know, they rang me.'

'Oh. Well. I'm sorry. About him. He's a tosser.'

'Yeah, I could have told you that.' I said, but I was smiling.

The guy laughed, but I could see how awkward he felt being so close to me. He looked around.

'Look, tell that guy, if you get the chance. If he's got a problem – to say it to my face!'

'Yeah. Yeah I will.'

He grinned, I felt better. He made to go, and I watched him walk back.

Nice guy. I thought. Not enough of those, clearly.

Then it hit me.

Was that Matt? Was he the mystery note writer?

Chapter 9 – Moving the car

It was always a welcome change in the evening when the temperature dropped down; I would take down any towels and fold and refold anything on the back seat. I did try to make the car look as presentable as I could by the afternoon. In a weird way I wanted Ryan to get back to something a little less depressing than the reality. An amusing habit, to feel house-proud of a tiny car that you and your love are living in. But it made me feel good, so I did it anyway.

I'd watch people drive away from their places of work and would imagine they were returning to their beautiful homes, with their heads full of ideas to have some chilled wine in their garden as the sun set. Or to soak away all the days worries in a bath. Or even to be greeted with a well-prepared meal. I missed food the most of everything in the car. I'd try not to think about it, but it was hard with nothing else to do. I'd dream up things I planned to cook for Ryan once we had a home of our own. Caesar salads with croutons and extra cheese, steak with thick cut chips and lashings of creamy peppercorn sauce. Stews in the winter. Doorstop white bread with crispy bacon and melting butter. My stomach growled in response. Easy now, easy now, Empty. I'll fill you again one day.

And not with fucking soup.

I felt immensely guilty that Ryan was working while I just sat here existing. I'd save my chocolate for him, and water too. Often, he'd get back and down the entire thing, having emptied his own early on. I'd read out my diary, or a chapter from a book I'd been given by a kindly old lady whilst with Ryan on his rounds.

Seeing his figure on the horizon brought the same relief I imagined all those people on their way home got from their evening baths, or glass of wine, or as they eased themselves into their fresh, clean sheets. It's a cliché but Ryan always brought the sense of home with him. Like a piece of me had been missing and now it was returned, and I was whole again.

The days in the car passed me by like a strange daydream. The moment Ryan was back in the car I couldn't disassociate myself from the day anymore and everything was brought into focus. Everything became real again, and we'd cling to each other wordlessly.

We were getting through this together.

I'd remind Ryan that in the grand scheme of our lives, this period would be a tiny blip. It wouldn't matter, not when it's over. It would be remembered until it became hazy, and then would become something that happened that we almost wouldn't believe, if not for the other reminding us. And I constantly told him, it will end. This is not forever.

I told him about the phone call from the police.

'Yeah, I know.' He sighed. 'They came to the depot to get a contact number, but I was out in the van. Lee wouldn't give them my work number so they must have given them this one to get rid of 'em.'

We agreed to find somewhere to ditch the car, permanently. Somewhere no one would notice us, and we'd be left to get ourselves out of this mess without anyone throwing another spanner in the works.

We moved the car at the weekend, despite what I had told the policewoman on the phone. A mile or so down the road was the Child Support Agency. The road stopped at some woodland, but there was a small lay-by/parking area that was deserted at the end of the week. We'd come across it by chance, and at a glance you wouldn't spot it. Which meant you wouldn't spot us. Which was exactly what we wanted.

There was a dog walking route, and at the weekend we'd been seen by some dog walkers, but generally they kept their heads down and out of our business, as we did theirs. That was the beauty of dog walking, most people would be occupied with their own thoughts, or whatever was going on in their own lives, or whether they had remembered poo bags or not. It was their chance to be alone with their thoughts, not poke their nose in where it wasn't wanted.

There was a gorgeous field to the right, once you walked through the tiny copse of trees. I'd explored it one weekend in the sunshine and found all kinds of trails through the wildflowers and brambles. It was like walking into an enchanted fairy land. I let my imagination run as wild as nature walking around there for a wonderful hour or two. I wondered if anyone else had found themselves looking for fairies there, although if they were, they'd be more likely to find me crouched behind some bushes having a nature wee.

We were nearly at the end of the month; it was a Friday and we had moved the car. Finally, we felt like there was some breathing room. The countdown was coming to an end.

 As much as it was hard and starting to feel hard on the both of us, the weekends still felt great- maybe it was because we were properly together, and we would go for a wander or find other ways to pass the time. We'd plan out loud the future, in the same way someone would plan their lottery win, and that's how it felt. Like once we had a proper roof over our heads, this nightmare would be over, and we'd have won the lottery – instead of money, we'd be winning the chance to continue a normal life, with everyone else. The end was nigh, we could feel it. This was all going to be over.

We wandered through the woodland that afternoon and came across a little village. A small hub with a corner shop and a pizza place. The smell of warm dough was too much.

'God, I want a pizza'

'Fucking - same.'

We hadn't had proper hot food in ages. One weekend we had bought a breakfast muffin at the café at Tesco, shared it between us, and it had been heavenly. But it was £4! That was our weekly budget. We'd shared it so equally, neither wanting to be the greediest. It had been such a test, especially with everyone around us tucking into full fry ups and leaving half of it behind. We didn't leave a single crumb or swipe of oil on that plate. You could have stuck it back on the shelf.

When we made our way back to the car, we opened our tins of soup and began to eat in silence.

'Oh, fuck this Ryan, it's shit!'

'I know... Could be worse though...'

'What is worse than tepid soup from a tin?' I laughed back at him

'Shit.'

We laughed together then. When dinner is only one up from actual shit, you have just got to laugh it off. We laughed loads thinking about it, despite everything. It's easy to feel shit when life seems to be going down the pan. But there is some positive to be found in everything. We might be in the car but at least we weren't on the street. We might be eating soup from a tin, but at least we were eating. We might have been forgotten about back home, but we still had each other.

Things would be ok, they would.

Wouldn't they?

Chapter 10 – The Job Centre

Before we were living out of the car, as I have mentioned, I had called the council to see what they could do. It was all I knew – if you find yourself homeless, ring the council and they will help you.

We had looked at our options, unsure of which route to go down. It had all felt so easy before we were here, living it. We looked at houses to rent, but with no stable jobs that was impossible. We looked at cheaper flats, hoping that maybe we'd find work and be able to pay the rent by the time it was due.

When that had failed, we looked at rooms to rent. But they were thin on the ground and often private advertisements we could afford were asking for single professional people. No couples. No DSS.

I didn't even know what 'No DSS' was, when I asked, I was told it was housing benefit.

I didn't know what housing benefit was either, so we looked it up at the library, needing to lie about being locals to get ourselves in. None of this stuff was taught to us, not in school, not as adults. There was a plethora of things available as 'safety nets' for people, but if we didn't know to ask – how could we ever access them?

'Sorry, there's nothing we can do, you aren't a Cornwall resident.'

Oh.

'But isn't there a duty of care?'

'You are intentionally homeless. We don't have a duty of care for you.'

Shit.

We were intentionally homeless. I had to agree. We'd really buggered it up this time. I wondered if people who were fleeing traumatic experiences were treated the same. Sadly, I imagined they were.

We needed a rethink. What were our other options?

Go back? Tails between our legs. Begging for forgiveness. I'm not sure Dad would even let us back. That man could hold a grudge for a century.

So then what?

Find housing, that is affordable? Impossible...

Jobs seemed to be non-existent down here, at least to anyone who wasn't a resident by birth. No one would take a chance on a couple with no fixed address.

So, we've fucked up. But how would we un-fuck ourselves?

We hadn't got any savings; Dad had charged us three quarters of our wages to live there, so he didn't have to work. And we weren't even allowed to watch TV. Or have a bath more than twice a week. Or use the kitchen.

Dad would never agree to write a letter to say we had been chucked out; not now. That safety net had been cut off long ago.

'Where are you sleeping tonight?' The council guy asked.

'On the beach, or in our car...' which had both been our options at that point. I wondered how many times they heard that one.

'Try the Job Centre. They may be able to help you with the money side of things.'

So, the appointment had rolled around, after a four week wait. We'd survived until now, so were ready for some good news, some help at last.

The appointment with an older lady, who asked us what we were doing to seek work. We told the truth – Ryan had found a job, and I didn't see the point in applying for jobs in an area we didn't plan to live in for much longer.

'We were hoping for a crisis loan, or something – to help us secure a flat. Then I was going to look for permanent work...so we could pay it back.'

She showed us to a computer room and told me I'd have to fill in an online form and begin to look for work, else I wouldn't be entitled to any help.

'This is a Jobseekers interview. Not a general enquiry.'

There hadn't been an option for anything other than that, I wanted to point out. But I didn't want to argue, so let her lead me into another small room.

The computer room was a tiny, stuffy office – only open at certain hours and I'd have to put my name down for an 'appointment' in there. If I was late or didn't show up, I wasn't allowed to use the room. I'd have to try again another day. But every day I would have to show that I had been actively looking for work. And I also wasn't allowed to turn down any opportunities that came up. An hour and a half commute each way, was deemed an acceptable distance I was expected to make should I be fortunate enough to find a job that far away. Whether I could afford to get myself there or not.

And I could not.

I was allocated 30 minutes internet time, and only permitted to use the computer to look for work. If I was found looking at anything not job search related, I'd be banned. So, I couldn't log in to Facebook to let anyone know where I was. Ryan had to wait outside; he wasn't allowed to sit next to me as it was one chair per computer.

A foreign lady next to me was trying to bid on council properties and getting confused with the system. I leant over to show her how to change the language to one she knew.

'Excuse me!'

There was a man overlooking everyone's computer, who was now barking at me. 'Focus on your OWN computer thank you!' He pointed at a sign that said exactly that, pursing his lips.

It if sounds oppressive, it was. I felt like I'd committed some sort of crime for not having a job. I'd found a job to apply for and began the online form. 'This application will take around 45 minutes to fill in.'

For fuck sake. I thought the job centre was meant to help you? Not hinder you at every opportunity.

I excused myself and left the room.

We had another appointment five minutes later with a woman to talk about a possible back payment of job seekers since we had been actively searching for so long and needed the money.

She explained there was an issue with our application, so we had to go through it with her. I carefully filled out every box and answered every question. I wrote as neatly as I could so there would be no mix ups. I presented the form to her carefully.

'You are to apply for a minimum of five jobs a week.'

'Ok.' It had been drummed into me enough times. 'But I'm struggling to apply for five a week because I can only use the computer for 30 minutes a day. Some applications take an hour to fill in properly, and no one takes a CV by hand anymore.'

'Don't you have use of the internet at home?' She rolled her eyes at my apparent excuses.

'I'm living in a car.' I told her. 'Until I have a-'

'You have no fixed address?'

'Well. No?'

'Without a fixed address you are not eligible for any benefit.'

She snatched the paperwork out of my hands and gestured with her hand for us to get up to leave.

'Nothing at all? How are we meant to-'?

'I'm afraid not. I do, however, have a leaflet ...for the soup run.'

She rustled around in a pile of paper to hand me a small print out of three different times a week that the soup run could be found. There was also a centre that homeless people could go to in the day for a hot meal, at the cost of £2.30.

I took the leaflet. More fucking soup.

'Thankyou.' I said, grimacing back at her. What a waste of time this had been.

'You are welcome. You can fill this out again once you are back on your feet...'

And with that, she ripped up the application form I had carefully filled in.

'Oh, the soup run does pasties as well!'

She said it so cheerfully I felt like I was having an out of body experience.

Oh, well that's great then, I'll just save up all the pasties and make myself a fucking pasty house. How were we ever supposed to get on our feet when every safety net we came across was being ripped up the moment we discovered it?

I suddenly realised why anyone becomes homeless in the first place. If either of us had more complex problems, well we'd have no hope. We'd been surviving on privilege and luck so far. But that seemed to be running out. And fast.

<u>Chapter 11 – The Dog Walker</u>

Since moving the car, Ryan had to get up even earlier, every day praying we'd stolen enough electricity to charge his phone for an alarm in the morning. The last thing we needed was for him to lose his job. I tried not to think about it, worried it might tempt a particularly cruel twist of fate.

His work provided a uniform which he'd take off and fold up the moment he got back every day, and we'd keep it as clean and tidy as we could. Looking at him, other than his now shaggy looking beard -you'd never really know we were living like this.

I felt safer now we were off the road, in our cosy corner. I'd keep the windows open and let myself relax. I'd write in my diary, kicking myself for filling it with pointless doodles now the pages were running out. I'd do that until I got bored. Then I'd try to keep my mind busy by remembering song lyrics and writing them down or drawing floor plans and furniture lists for our flat. I heard about The Law of Attraction, and hoped by telling myself it would be ours, that positive thinking would make it so.

One afternoon I peered through the wing mirrors – the car was parked with its nose to the bushes, it just felt more private that way – when I spotted an elderly lady walking her dog past the car.

'Oh disgusting. This is. Disgusting!' She spat out her words. I looked around at what she was seeing.

There was rubbish strewn into the hedges nearby. It had been there when we arrived, plastic bottles and toilet roll. Wrappers and beer cans. Even a pizza box and a few nappies. I'd stopped noticing it by now, I'd even picked up what I could reach and taken it to Tesco to put in the bins there. It wasn't us throwing rubbish into the bushes, but I realised it would probably look that way.

Still. It wasn't me. And I'd made the effort to clean it up as much as I could, but because I was clearly living in the car, this woman had put two and two together and clearly gotten five.

Well, I wasn't taking the blame this time.

She was grumbling away as she walked around the car, not giving me eye contact.

'Absolutely vile. A disgrace. Should be ashamed...'

Well. I'm not proud of it, dear reader.

But I chased her.

I chased an old lady down the street.

And her dog.

She didn't look behind her at first but started walking more briskly, then jogging to get away from my thundering footsteps behind her. I used to win the 100 metres at school lady, you ain't going to outrun me! As I began closing in, my long legs no match for her aged old twiglets, she took a quick turn through the copse of trees, the darkness stealing her from my sight.

Oh god. I thought as I pushed through the trees, still chasing her. Anger still pulsing through me as each step hit the ground. She didn't know what this was like. She didn't try to understand how scary this all was. I was running on adrenaline every day, and not just here – at 'home' too. Life probably just passed her by, opportunities falling in her lap. She probably had a husband at home, a lovely garden, her stupid dog thinking she was the most wonderful human on the planet. And what did we have? Nothing.

She didn't know how we'd already been threatened from the business estate, how we worried about the police deciding to move in and take our car. How the job centre had shunned us, the council had shrugged at us. How Ryan was working so hard to keep our heads above water, and she was soaring past in her yacht judging us and letting her judgement wash over our attempts to survive.

She didn't know. But it wouldn't have been hard to hazard a guess. To allow us some empathy. To accept that things probably weren't great for us right now.

So, I chased her. And I yelled. And if I had caught up with her, I'd have probably punched her in the hunch.

I could still her mumbling as she went out of view. Rage coursed through my veins as I squinted through the trees. I shouted after her - 'Shut your fucking face!'

Well, that wasn't my finest moment. If she hadn't thought I was scum, she certainly did now.

******

When a policeman turned up that evening, I have to say, surprise was not my first emotion.

I had told Ryan about what had happened, he laughed and told me he'd have probably done the same.

'We could have chased her together!' I laughed wickedly.

Of course, we wouldn't have.

Then a police-car pulled up behind us, and our laughing stopped abruptly.

'Omm...They are definitely here for you.' Ryan whispered.

The policeman popped his head around the window and asked me what was going on. Embarrassed, I politely explained the situation. The usual, we just don't have anywhere to stay right now, but Ryan had work nearby so we were waiting to get a flat deposit together. I told him it was just temporary, that we'd soon be out of Plymouth all together.

He nodded in reply.

'Hmm. Ok. Right.'

He took my details but made no mention of any shouting at old ladies. I figured I wouldn't either. It wasn't lying, it was just omission of the entire facts.

He seemed entirely unbothered by our situation, as though we really had just happened to park up there five minutes beforehand. I just hoped he would bugger off and leave us be.

'Gylisa? Do you want to take this?'

He handed me a card, I looked at him properly now, allowing him to become human to me. I realised then that I'd been keeping myself separate from other people deliberately. His eyes were soft and kind.

'It's my number. My police number.' He corrected himself.

'If anyone gives you any trouble, give me a ring. Do you have a phone?'

'We do.'

'Good. Take care guys, Good luck,'

We thanked him and watched him leave. I spotted another security guard stood at the end of the carpark across the road. Watching us.

I felt weird. Being constantly on edge was no good for my body, and even when darkness fell, my shoulders didn't unclench. If I felt like this, I wondered how Ryan must be feeling.

The more interaction we had with people the more I felt like I was drifting off the edges of accepted society. Like I was no longer normal and behaving in the accepted norms didn't have to apply to me anymore. A small part of me felt like I wasn't welcome back, that perhaps we would be destined to always live on the outside. Maybe we were just 'outsiders'.

Dad had called me lazy, and now I felt it. I felt like all the insults anyone had ever called me or had ever aimed at anyone who was homeless or jobless or deemed as 'less than' were finally sinking into my skin. It all felt true. How could I prove otherwise? I was all those things. Look where it had gotten me.

I just felt ashamed that I'd dragged Ryan into it with me. He deserved better, I thought.

I still couldn't help but notice that no one from home had made any effort to see where I had disappeared to. Not mum, or dad. My brother or sister. Not even any of my close friends. Or even the people I'd drink with in the pub.

No one had noticed. Perhaps I hadn't been as important as I thought? Perhaps I'd just added to the numbers. Been another face in a photo. Another person to get a round of drinks in. Thinking about it I don't remember any of them asking how I was and really meaning it. I was invited out for a good time, that was my purpose.

A melancholy loneliness began to creep in. Was this how people felt before they killed themselves? I felt like it probably was. If I hadn't had Ryan with me I might have even seen it as an option.

But Ryan and I had been bickering the last few evenings too. He kept telling me to go home and wait until he had sorted things, and I kept refusing. I couldn't go just go home. Where would I go to? There wasn't anywhere to go to. Not now.

And besides, how could I go back knowing he was left to face the days by himself. If we were going to get through this, we were going to do it together. That was the deal.

That had been the dream. The hard times might be here right now, but the good times will come again.

They always do – don't they?

Chapter 12 – The Stars

I was starting to hit a low period. I had tried so hard to keep spirits high, but now I was running on empty.

There was an undercurrent of blame running through the atmosphere, and while I didn't hear him say it – I felt that Ryan would never have been in a situation like this if it weren't for me. He'd have continued with his first job, going out with the lads. Training hard. He might have even competed as a physique model by now. Instead I'd dragged him into my life, and the downward spiral I was on. Now he was fighting to keep us afloat. The guilt and shame of it burned through me.

I raised the subject one evening, trying to break the silence. We had gone from chatting about our days, however boring - to conversations about anything and everything...

Now a heavy silence filled the car, and I do not work well in silence. Dad used silence as punishment, knowing that the unseen pressure would do enough damage that he needn't waste his breath. My ex-boyfriend had used silence, radio silence, disappearing for hours when he had promised to turn up at a certain time. He'd turn up hours later, drunk and ask me why I was getting so upset?

He'd ignore phone calls or texts, reminding me every day – I'd be spoken to when he chose it. Not before. It created such a heavy atmosphere that I felt physically squashed under it, needing some words, any words to break through it so I could breathe again.

And now here I was again, stuck in silence.

Ryan thought for a moment, and then told me I should go home, again.

'I don't want to go home.'

No matter what scrapes we would get ourselves in as kids, my friends always had the option of just going home. Mum and Dad = safety. Like the Winchester, my friends could escape and wait 'for all this to blow over'. Whatever the sitch, once inside their homes they were untouchable again. A lighthouse from the storm.

For me, whatever chaos was ensuing outside of my home I could guarantee it was less scary than anything going on inside it.

And now I'd taken the chance to run away from it, there was no way I could ever just turn up again. Going back was impossible. It wasn't an option.

I hadn't come this far to only get this far.

 I had done that once before and I swore as I walked up that road and Dads house loomed into view, that I would never return if I had another chance.

After Mum had escaped from Dads and left us behind, she promised me she'd come back for me, and then, when I was 17, she did. She pressed a key into my hand and told me the address, a road away from Dad's house.

I'd ran down to it that evening, opening the tiny cottage door and walking into what was going to be our new home. Just me and mum. Mum and me.

The smell of paint hung in the air; the walls all painted magnolia. I'd carefully walked around the small cottage, marvelling at the Victorian fireplaces. Peering through the windows. Overjoyed with the feeling of finally, finally having somewhere safe, and clean and homely.

Mum claimed child benefit for me, and one morning the postman pushed through what seemed like hundreds of cheques, they fell through the letterbox like a waterfall of money. We couldn't believe it!

We cashed them in, and went on a spree to Ikea, filling the car so full we didn't have room to move, and we certainly weren't legal on the road. But we did it and made it home. Our home.

A few weeks later, Mum moved her new boyfriend in. It wasn't me and mum anymore. It was Mum and Brad, and then me trailing behind. An extra mouth to feed. Things got awkward. It wasn't that I didn't like him, he *was* really nice, it was that I didn't like who Mum was when she was with him. We never seemed to have any money, and when we did – it never lasted long. Mum would cook dinner for two and act surprised when I walked in.

She ended up so stressed about money that they came up with an idea.

'We can't afford to live here anymore. So, we're going to save up, to buy a canal boat.'

So, the saving began. Everyone that would pop in for a cuppa was talked into dropping a quid or two into the huge jar. Everyone was happy to help, Mum had never asked for anything before, and our friends all knew she'd drop a quid in should they need it. And if she had it.

The trouble was, I often had no money to get to college, or for something to eat. So would sneak a few quid back out, promising I'd put it back in.

Nevertheless, despite my borrowing, the day finally came, and with a deposit for a bank loan. The boat was bought.

'What will my bedroom be like on the boat, Mum?'

'Er- why don't you come along and see for yourself?'

So, I did. The boat they'd picked was at a boat yard, so we drove down to have a look. I chattered away the entire drive, telling Mum how I'd help decorate it, and that we'd keep it all vintage styled, because that was the nicest.

We got there, and it was huge! Much bigger than I'd imagined, and excitedly, I'd jumped onboard.

This was our new, new home then!

I passed through the living area, poking my head into the toilet/shower room. There was one bedroom that had a door, which lead into, I opened it tentatively...

An engine room.

Hang on.

'Where will I sleep Mum?' I asked her, confused.

'Ah. Well. About that...'

Mum explained that there wasn't going to be any room for me on the boat permanently. That I'd be welcome to stay on their sofa bed in the living space, from time to time.

We drove back to the cottage and I was quiet.

Where was I going to go then? I tried to add up the bills in my head, hoping that I could quit college and get a job and stay here, in this cottage. I'd be eighteen next year, so it shouldn't be a problem. If I could afford it. But Mum was struggling, even with her boyfriend living here. And I needed money now.

'Look, Gee. I've spoken to your Dad, and he's cooked you some dinner.' Mum said, as we walked through the door.

'You might want to go up there, and make amends...'

I replayed the shouting. Fighting. Dad throwing my things out on the lawn, for what I had assumed was the final time.

I thought about myself, taking his clothes and scattering them out the window. My last act of defiance. The first one of us to stick it to him. I'd done that because I thought I would never go back.

And now I had no choice.

I'd carried what little belongings I had back up the road to Dads house that evening, alone.

Home sweet home.

****

'I can stay here, keep working, wait until I've been paid and then once we have somewhere to go you can come back. And we can start from there...'

I realised Ryan saw this as his mess, and his responsibility to get us out of it. He couldn't be more wrong. Tears filled my eyes.

The pressure he must be feeling must be tenfold of the silence.

It's true, everything was riding on Ryan working and being paid.

I remembered working, before the office job. Eighteen years old and working full time. I'd began as a waitress, before becoming the manager of two restaurants, simultaneously. I remembered every hard hour, every back-breaking moment of cleaning, of customer service, organising a team of people, most of whom were older than me, and it had all felt worth it when I saw a comma in my bank balance. And I knew I could piss it all up the wall if I wanted. Most of the time, I did. It beat going home, that's for sure.

It was the reward for working hard, what a concept now! Even working in the call centre, every single person sat at their desk, with their snacks and their social media and everything else within arm's reach, they had said how *hard they worked* for a living. What an absolute joke that was now, in this heat, in this car. Waking up before the birds. And for what? Minimum wage. If the company was legally allowed to pay less, they surely would.

Ryan's reward for working so hard didn't exist. It was just survival. This was hard work that most people couldn't even imagine. They'd have a shock if they could, that's for sure.

I leaned into him and squeezed his arm.

'I'm not leaving you Ryan.'

He closed his eyes for a moment, brow furrowed in thought. Guilt. Shame. Stress.

'Ryan,' I squeezed his arm again. 'We are in this together. We will get out of it together too.' He shook his head.

'I just feel shit. I want to make you happy. But look where we are...'

'I am happy' I promised him.

'I'm with you.'

****

As darkness encased us, the last cars left the vicinity, and the comforting peace of knowing we were alone again shrouded the car. I rested my head against the cold glass window and noticed the sky was completely clear.

'Ryan...look...' I pointed upwards, excited. 'You can see all the stars!'

I pulled him out the car to sit on the kerb and gaze with me. He complained, said his back was hurting and it was cold. But he let me drag him out anyway and looked up at the display.

Every single star seemed to be fighting to be noticed first. It was astonishing. The first time we'd sat out and enjoyed the view.

I pointed out all the constellations I knew. I settled on my favourite – Orion's belt, and as I leaned against Ryan's solid form, he told me it was his favourite too.

'It doesn't matter that things are shit now.' I told him. 'It just means the only way is up.'

He reached for my hand and held it, and for that moment, we weren't down on our luck, we weren't living in the car. We were just two people, who loved each other and were lucky enough to have the stars twinkling above us. Nothing else was important for now. Dare I say, I felt lucky to be here for the first time.

A twig crunched behind us, and we turned to see two dog walkers, hand in hand walking straight through our moment. Two springer spaniels jumped between us, the guy walking behind them shouting 'OI!'

He saw us then and narrowed his eyes.

'Ain't you got nowhere to live?' He barked at us. Seeing the car and putting two and two together. He was a rough looking man, the sort of guy who'd have his nickname tattooed on his arm, in case he forgot it.

'No.' I spoke for us; Ryan was awkward, having not had this conversation before and avoided it by petting the dog.

'Well, don't you have a job?'

'Obviously not.' I shrugged. If he was going to act like an idiot, then I may as well treat him like one.

His girlfriend was smirking at us. Was this so amusing? I felt not, but then again, I wasn't seeing our situation through their eyes. Defensive, because of that rude old woman, I was ready to argue, Hell – I was ready to chase these two off as well.

But he left it at 'Oh.' And walked off.

Still in earshot, he and his girlfriend began talking about us, as though we weren't there. Trailing off as they got further away. Humiliation coursed through me, but I knew Ryan was feeling it so much worse.

I could push through those feelings; I'd felt them often enough. Humiliation at my house, my parents, my clothes, at school. But Ryan had never been on this side of humiliation before. It stung.

'Fucks sake.' He muttered, voice cracking.

I cringed after him, not sure how to spin this into a positive. I'd just have to try.

Chapter 13- The Tuna Pasta

It was Friday!

Fridays were always good because it meant we had two uninterrupted days of each other. Plus, on this Friday, we were planning to walk to the Life Centre and have a swim. It was £7 for the two of us, and we'd been careful with our money to allow a much-needed wash and I personally felt reborn once I'd scrubbed my skin pink.

Ryan's beard had grown so much now, I'd never seen him with so much facial hair. But it was out of control, messy and when he wasn't in his work clothes, he looked like the sort of person who you'd avoid on the bus, and not be surprised whatsoever should he reveal a nest of mice living in there.

Not washing didn't bother me too much, I had had my baths rationed sparingly my entire life. But for Ryan it was a form of torture. He liked to start every day fresh, so we'd stretched our budget to a roll-on deodorant and some packets of baby wipes. But Life Centre day always put Ryan in a great mood.

After we had swam and showered and cleaned everything we could. I cleaned my shoes with loo roll, we even brought nail clippers! I felt so clean my skin felt see through. Ryan had packed our bags and we sat in the park outside the building for a while. Normal again. No one shooting furtive glances towards us. No one whispering to their friend as they walked past. No one staring at our bags, or shoes or anything. We were normal, and invisible in the best way possible. Just one face in a sea of many. Back into the comfort zone.

Ryan likes going under the radar. He likes choosing when he wants attention and is happy to let it slide past him when he doesn't. I spent half my life being the ugly sister, then the ugly friend, then the weird kid. I mean, yeah, I had plenty of friends, but I was invisible for a long time, until one day I didn't want to be invisible anymore, and people stopped looking without seeing.

Mum always made comments about walking with me around town. 'I love walking around with you, everyone stares at you Gee, don't you notice?' Truthfully, I didn't anymore. I thought people stared at everyone.

'They never look at me, unless I'm with you.' Mum told me, half proud, half jealous.

I didn't really believe her, until the first day I'd walked into that call centre, for my interview, the entire call floor went quiet. It was only for a moment. But if you have ever visited a call centre you will know how loud they can be. I allowed myself to be impressed for a moment, it had never happened before after all.

I was always aware that this feeling doesn't last forever. I suppose that's what you learn when you grow up ugly. Personality counts for more, and I had worked on both. I knew when my looks did fade, well – I'd better be able to look in the mirror and still be proud of the person I was seeing in it.

Now outside the Life Centre, sat in the sunshine. I was invisible again. No more interesting than the grass growing beside me. And that was fine by me.

****

When we got back to the car, I began to read to Ryan. He was getting into my charity shop books which I enjoyed, because he said he didn't like to read, and I felt like it was such a waste. Books had taught me everything I hadn't be taught from life itself. They'd been my escape whenever things had been bad. And I wanted to take him through the trapdoor of a book, so he could have his mind taken away from our surroundings.

When I read, I stop seeing the words, everything around me just melts away and there I am, within the pages of the book, experiencing all the highs and lows with the characters inside. Reading is like watching a film in your head. But you get to choose the cast and the back drops.

Ryan would lie back, eyes closed, and I would begin to read. I couldn't tell if he was listening or not, but it was something to do, so on I read.

Just as we were getting into it, a van came speeding up the road, straight through our joint daydream and swerved around us.

'Oh shit.'

Two men jumped out, tanned lads, wearing vests. It was only as they got closer, I realised it was the guy from the other day. The rough looking guy with the dogs!

He knocked on Ryan's window.

'Alright?' He asked loudly. Shouted it, really. We were too taken aback to answer. He didn't wait for a reply.

'We brought you some hot pasta...'

He showed us a Tupperware container, full of steaming hot pasta and tuna.

Ryan opened his window, mouth agape. Unsure how to say thank you for such a gesture.

The man shook it all off, passing in the lunchbox, with two plastic spoons and a packet of jam tarts.

'T-Thankyou. Really. You didn't have to do this...'

Even I was stammering out my words, I just couldn't believe it.

'It's no trouble. We just thought you might appreciate something warm; it's getting colder out now...'

We knew. We'd spent a few evenings shivering now. And we did appreciate it, we told him. We were so grateful! Neither of us could believe it!

'I'll come back for the box, so don't worry about it...' He said, still in his harsh tone. I guessed that's just how he speaks. With that, he and his son, we guessed, got back in the van and drove off.

We opened the Tupperware immediately and a puff of steam came out, inside was a huge portion of tuna pasta, with creamy sauce and melted cheese glistening over it – it smelt divine. We wasted no time staring at it and got stuck in.

'It's probably laced with drugs' Ryan laughed in between great mouthfuls.

'Who cares!' I said. 'Free drugs!'

'At least we'd get a good night's sleep!'

'Yeah...-And we'll wake up tomorrow morning, naked, in the foetal position, one less kidney each...'

'Those kind bastards have fleeced us!' Ryan finished and we grinned at each other.

Turns out - one portion of tuna pasta, followed rapidly by two jam tarts each – would be just the thing to lift our spirits. Not only that but we were clean, our bellies were fuller than they'd been in weeks. And as we pulled the duvet over us that night before darkness fell – we felt like the luckiest, homeless people in Plymouth.

****

The next morning, I woke up not hungry for the first time since we'd arrived in Cornwall. That, and the Tupperware on the back seat reminded me of last night's kindness, which made me think about our family and friends.

The kindness of one stranger had been so immense that it left me wondering if I was right about not having a home to go back to. Maybe I'd got it wrong, not everyone was so bad. Perhaps I had a flawed perspective, and I was simply thinking the worst of them. And they didn't even know where we were. Was I wrong?

But how do you tell the people you love that you aren't ok, actually?

I'd read homeless statistics before. Not to toot my own horn, but I'd even bought a Big Issue during our first week in Cornwall.

Seriously though, I liked to buy them and learn a little more about it all. Now I felt like I was a few weeks away from selling it myself. And I'd need money for that too, nothing was free.

I'd read how many homeless people simply ran out of sofas to sleep on, floors to occupy. Some of them are too proud to ask for help so disappear. Offers run out eventually, if you don't get yourself brushed off quickly enough. And then just like that you become a burden. That was a feeling I knew all too well. I was reminded often enough. Come back from school, can't have anything to eat because it costs money. Don't need new shoes because it all costs money. Can't use the washing machine because it costs too much money. Can't have a bath because it costs, too, much, money.

I didn't want to be a burden to anyone else in my life, not now, not ever.

Besides, everyone else has their own stuff going on, I don't want to make them worry. It's not permanent. I tell myself again, like it's become our mantra.

It's not permanent, even if it feels like it is.

Just like that I talk myself out of making the phone call. There's no sense in worrying them. It isn't permanent. I'll call them when we are back on our feet.

They would only worry.

Chapter 14 – The Trip to Plymouth

It was the end of the month.

Go time.

We'd hashed out a plan over the weekend, and I'd written and rewritten it in my diary enough times.

The plan was as follows, I had £5 in change which I was going to use to get the bus into Plymouth. Once there, I would go to the bank with Ryan's card and withdraw what we would need for a deposit. After that, I would get the train to Liskeard, walk to the estate agents and give them the cash, securing the place as ours and then! We would have somewhere to live in a few days' time.

Sorted.

Ryan left for work that day, excited for the first time – ever.

He kissed me as he left and wished me luck.

I didn't need it, I told myself; I was ready to put an end to this hell. The nights were getting colder, we were getting hungrier. Dirtier, and we were fucking fed up.

The tuna pasta had been such a lovely way to end this journey. But we couldn't rely on handouts and kindness for the rest of our time here.

So, now it was all going to be over, I didn't care if we had to wait a week for the contract to be finalised, once I knew what day we could move in, I could count down the days, minutes and seconds. It was going to be over.

This was going to be our tiny blip. Insignificant! Forgotten about! A footnote in the story of our lives.

We had been so careful, making sure our money would last until today, knowing it wouldn't stretch a day over. After this there was none. We'd saved a jam tart each, although they were looking a little ropey. But beggars can't be choosers. Our jam tart contingency. At least we'd staved off rickets for the last few weeks.

I got half dressed in the car, standing outside of it to brush my clothes straight and comb my hair into a more reasonable shape. It didn't matter if I was a little rough around the edges, as long as the estate agents' immediate thought wasn't 'She is living rough, therefore not reliable, do *not* rent to her.'

The lady working there had already seemed to be a total snob, she had an air about her, like a teacher who hasn't taken a liking to you, looking us up and down when we walked in, as though we may have just walked dog shit through the office- instead of greeting us.

So, I couldn't afford to have anything work against us.

I smoothed my clothes down, I felt homeless, but I wasn't sure I really *looked* it. My hair was brushed, although looked dull. My face was wet wiped clean. I kept my fingernails short so they wouldn't gather dirt – long gone were the days of my monthly acrylics.

I looked at my hands for a moment, and realised I didn't miss that. My hands were tanned now, a sprinkle of freckles across the back. Many a day spent with the sun bouncing off the sea had done that. A million miles away from my nails clicking against a keyboard, hands pale under a glaring artificial light.

It was just a small thing to notice, but it made me feel beauty in amongst the bad. Sure, I was homeless – but look how tanned I am. Ooh....

I gathered a bag ready, watching my hands stuff everything in - wallet, car keys, phone, baby wipes. And off I went.

Tesco first, to check the bank.

I had to squint at the screen and lean close to it to make out the numbers, pressing in the pin carefully. The machine whirred. I was trying to guess how much should be in there, maths not being my strong point, now or ever. But I was sure it should be at least £1000. Enough for the deposit, fees and a month's rent. With almost nothing left over. But we'd agreed – once we had an address, we would qualify for help, finally.

The only way was up from there.

The display came up, and I peered down at it.

£-00.12

Fuck.

The colour drained from my face.

My legs prickled with goose bumps and a surge of nausea churned in my stomach as I tried to make sense of it. No. Have we got the days wrong? Is it not in yet? Is there a mistake we have overlooked?

I couldn't see any transactions because it wasn't a cash point that did that. All I could get was a receipt. I couldn't go into the actual bank because I wasn't Ryan. My mind was going a million miles an hour and coming back to the same question each time.

What are we going to do?

There was a queue at the bus stop, and I felt uncomfortable because I was still without contact lenses and couldn't see much further than an arm's length away. Buses make me nervous, so I felt highly strung anyway. I held my sweaty change in my pocket, knowing I couldn't afford to lose a penny of it, although I was probably making it grossly warm for the driver. Ahh well, even homeless - I bet my hands are cleaner than his.

A bus pulled up and a few people got off, someone knocked into me roughly, so I dropped my bag. The queue moved without me as I scooped my belongings back in. God's sake, I hate buses. I hate public transport. I hate this. What was I going to do? Should I still go into the city? Maybe the cash was delayed. It might have gone in if I check another cash point.

Someone tapped me on the shoulder.

'Excuse me miss?'

An old guy was talking to me, I tried not to squint at him.

'I've got an all-day travel ticket – it was cheaper, but I only needed it until now. Don't tell the driver, but you can use it if you like?'

He held out the ticket. I stared at him.

Are you an angel?

'You can travel anywhere in these zones with it, return journeys too.'

'Um. Thankyou.'

What a stroke of luck. It's always there when you need it. Suddenly, my pocket change was safe. I could buy lunch!

My thoughts were going a million miles an hour. I thanked the guy again and stepped onto the bus. The driver nodded at the ticket, and pulled away, destination – Plymouth city centre. But first, my destination was an old lady's lap, because the bus lurched forward before I was ready and I skidded right into her.

The second I stepped off the bus I was on a mission, find another cash point and check the money. I had to make sure. I didn't want to waste a single second of time; I was praying to be back before Ryan, so he didn't have to wait for the good news.

I found one, slid Ryan's card in and waited, heartbeat drumming in my ears.

-00.12

For fucks sake. Now I couldn't deny it, the money wasn't there.

The money wasn't there.

How was I going to tell Ryan?

'There's no help available.' The job centre women's voice rang in my ears. 'You are intentionally homeless.' I heard the council guy say again.

I shut my eyes for a moment and kicked the wall. This is all my fault. I wanted to begin wailing it out loud. We are going to have to find the soup run. We might have to beg for money. My eyes quickly scanned the floor just in case, but I couldn't see further than my own feet and the feeling of doom washed through me even more.

We are fucked.

Were we fucked?

I sat down on a bench and ran my fingers through my hair. Think.

What can I do? I don't want to waste this trip. I certainly can't afford to do this again, even with that guys all day travel ticket.

Maybe I was meant to come to Plymouth, but what for? What could I do now? I didn't want to waste the £5 cash that I had. It really was all WE had now. Until when? Who knows?

I dropped my bag next to me and a reflection caught my eye. Ryan's iPod.

I'd forgotten all about that, having not used or needed my handbag for weeks. Ryan had suggested selling it ages ago, reasoning that we weren't going to be using it, so we might as well. I'd argued not to at that point. It was full of songs from our teenage years, memories and happy associations.

 How depressing.

But now, we were up the proverbial creek, again. I reckoned I'd get at least £30 for it. It was in great condition. And we could eek out £30 for a month. We'd done it once. We could survive. Just like that, my trip had a purpose. I made my way to Cash Converters.

A loud girl stepped into my path, I'd been walking on the outskirts of everyone else, head down, trying to be invisible. She'd obviously seen me, ignored the vibe and plopped herself in front of me. I squinted at her, she was wearing a bright t-shirt, and I vaguely saw several others wearing the same ones. Selling tactics. They were street selling, insurance, or dogs trust, or some charity. Well jog on sis, because I *am* a charity case. I didn't care what their sales tactic was, I just wanted to try and feed Ryan and me.

'Free doughnut?!'

'What?'

She brandished a tiny plastic bag, holding one powdery doughnut, the catch? – a leaflet stapled to it detailing whatever it was that was paying her to be bothering me.

'Free doughnut! With every leaflet! Take one!' She pushed it onto me, before I could think about it, and then I realised what had happened, and asked her for another. I'd save that for Ryan, I thought. She shrugged and crushed it into my hand.

Pleased with my luck today, minus the sentence to homelessness for another month at least. A doughnut will soften the blow.

I hope.

****

Cash converters smells like feet.

I had never been in one before, which made me feel slightly middle class compared to everyone else queuing up to sell their crap, until I realised that I was exactly like them. If not worse. I'm still selling my stuff because I need the money. I looked at the items for sale with a tag about saying 'Pre-loved' or 'pre-owned.' It wasn't selling for that cheap, which buoyed my nerves greatly. They must have bought it for a good price then.

As I had never been in a Cash Converters before, I didn't know how it all worked. Would they ask for proof of purchase? I didn't have that. What if they knew it wasn't mine to be selling? I might know Ryan was ok with it being sold, but they might think I've stolen it. What if they take it off me altogether?

I made out a sign that said 'Selling' with two empty till spaces and waited there.

A guy appeared. He looked like the kind of person who works in IT, and seemed to be the source of the foot smell.

'Can I help?'

He sounded sarcastic, like I was clearly beyond all help as in I was in here, but I didn't work here, so who was the real loser? He didn't have to know I'd come here from a car, which also happened to be my house. I was polite regardless.

'I was wondering if I could sell this?'

I passed him the iPod, noticing for the first time in the stark light how scratched and battered looking it really was. He turned it over in his hands, inspecting the charging point and headphone jack. I bit my lip.

'I'll have to test it first. Will take me five minutes. Take this receipt, and I'll see you then.' He handed me a receipt once printed and I took my cue to go.

With no way of knowing the exact time, I hung around outside for a moment, the sunlight obnoxiously brighter than the shop had been. I half-heartedly counted five minutes or so and made my way back in.

'Do you have the charger?'

'Um...no.'

I wasn't sure if that was the right answer or not, would he assume I've stolen it without it? Would he refuse to buy it?

'I've got the headphones...' I offered lamely.

'We don't sell the headphones with it, just the charger. Without the charger its worth....; He clicked his tongue, still turning the iPod over in his greasy hands.

'Ten quid.'

Ten shitty quid? I can't go back with a stale doughnut, no iPod, no hope but a tenner.

'Would you like to sell?' He pressed.

Ten pounds. Something special turned into ten fucking pounds.

But what was the alternative? I couldn't come back if Ryan said I should have sold it.

'Yeah. I'll sell. Thanks.'

He pressed the note into my hand and gave me another receipt, and walked off, flipping Ryan's iPod in his hand. Just another bit of junk to him, I guess.

I made my way back through town, bought some chips and did not feel good.

As I waited for the bus to take me back to the car, back to reality. I saw people sat in the bars outside laughing and smoking. That was me once. Not so long ago. Pink wine and a pack of Benson & hedges. Marlboro lights if I was feeling snobby. Cocktail cigarettes if I was feeling fancier still. I didn't even like the taste of them; they were just pretty.

At 5pm, I got on the bus, and it began to rain. I made my way back to the car from the bus stop, letting my hair get soaked, seeing it as a free wash.

Every hour that passed was an hour closer to telling Ryan the bad news.

I sat with my eyes closed listening to the sound of rain hitting the car. I'd left Ryan's phone in here, so I could call it from a payphone if I was still in Liskeard at 7pm. Oh, how different the day had turned out.

I willed the time away, enjoying the smell of sea water on the warm tarmac. Ignoring the faint smell of piss the rain was kicking up from getting caught short in the middle of the night. I opened my eyes to race raindrops against each other on the windshield when the phone rang loudly.

I scrabbled around for it, reading the name flashing up.

Gee's Mum.

'Hello?'

'G!'

She sounded jolly and excited to hear my voice. I hadn't realised how long it had been since I had spoken to her.

'What's going on then? We haven't heard from you! What are you up to?'

I couldn't lie. Not just because she's my mum – I can't lie to anyone. So, I told her how it was. I said we'd camped a few places in Cornwall and run out of money. That Ryan had a job and was meant to be paid today so we could get a flat, but it hadn't happened. I even told her about the free doughnuts. I left out the tuna pasta. I didn't want her to worry too much.

'Oh Gee, well what can we do? I haven't got much money. How much will you need to tide you over?'

I didn't know. I didn't know how much was not much. And it felt rude to ask, even if she was my mum.

'Give me your bank details and I'll put £80 in. Don't want to think of you starving out there...'

'Thanks mum. Thankyou. I'll pay you back as soon as we have some money back in.

I gave her my details and thanked her over and over. She faffed and found a pen and promised me it would be in there within the hour.

'Got to go now, but I love you! Bye!'

She hung up and I held the phone still for a moment. I missed her. I missed my mum. I didn't know how else to express it, but she was my *mum*. I missed her faffing and her voice and her presence. I felt like a tiny child again, who just wanted a hug with her mummy.

I knew if I told her that things were awful, and we were starving and not sure what to do she'd have told us to come back. She'd have told us to get the petrol and just hope we didn't get pulled over before we were in Gloucestershire.

But we were so close still. We were going to make it, I could feel it. Even if no one else could.

Chapter 15- Back at the start.

Ryan got back.

I broke the news of the money not being there and held him while he went through all the emotions I had. He kept asking me 'What are we going to do now?' But what could I say? I didn't know.

I didn't know. I had thought about it for hours and then some and then thought about it some more while he made a ropey phone call with the last of our phone battery. He called his boss and asked what was going on, his boss told him that he had to work a month in hand. So, it would be two months until he would get any money. It felt like a life sentence.

Two months.

Ryan asked if he could have an advance, but his boss told him he should have asked at the start of the month for that, now it wouldn't be possible. Ryan sank back into his chair.

'I spoke to my mum earlier. She sent some money over. Shall we at least check to see if that money has gone in?'

He nodded and we walked in silence to Tesco to check the bank.

The money was in. As mum had promised. I felt guilty for doubting it.

Mum had suggested buying a camping kettle, and a stove. 'There'll be a camping section, its summer!' And she told me to get whatever else, and don't feel guilty. 'You're a survivor G, like me.'

We were in the camping aisle now, but it was all so expensive. I found a tiny kettle, and a single 'ring' camping stove. We picked up two mugs, teabags, sugar, and some UHT milk. Gosh, it had been weeks since we'd be able to drink tea when we felt like it.

Then we bought more tins of things, anything but soup – we were sick to death of the stuff. We even treated ourselves to some bread, and chocolate too. We picked up some more water, then went to charge the phone and have a sink wash.

Once it was all paid for, we carried everything back to the car and had our first cup of tea.

It wasn't normal, but it was our normal. For now.

'Gutted about my iPod.'

'I'm sorry. I thought it was the right thing to do at the time. I had no idea Mum would give us some cash. So that's that gone forever.'

'I would have done the same, and I did say you could! It's just a shame isn't it?'

We drank our tea from our new mugs and relaxed. This whole situation was a shame. At least we've got a cup of tea though. Tea makes everything seem alright.

Ryan looked at.

'How do you do it, G?'

'What?'

'Stay so upbeat about it all?'

I shrugged.

'Most people would cry at this situation. But you…Well, you take pride in wet wiping the dashboard like it's a state-of-the-art kitchen…'

We laughed at the thought. I did do that, yes. But what was the alternative? Feel like shit, live in shit?

I wanted to be house-proud. Er, car-proud.

'I just don't ever feel like it's really 'over'. Y'know?'

'No. I don't know.' Ryan admitted, drinking his tea. 'I shit myself every day that this is permanent.'

'But something always happens to save the day. Doesn't it?!'

He made a non-committal grunt, unsure if I was exactly right.

'Look, we made it to Cornwall. Didn't we?'

'Yeah. And now we are living out of a car like two vagabonds…' He raised his eyebrows.

'We ran out of money, yeah. But then a job came up.'

'A shit job, that is hard work for fuck all pay.'

'But it's better than nothing!' I mused.

'We've not lost the car, even though we could have. We've got each other. We've even got cups of tea!' I held my cup up cheerily. 'What else could we ask for?!'

Ryan looked at me, amused at my optimism. Chuckling at my logic.

'So, we are in the car for another month then?' He asked.

'Yep. Another month.'

The countdown had reset itself.

Just another 28 days to go.

****

Once we had accepted that we weren't going to be leaving the car anytime soon, we just knuckled back down and got on. Like I said, there's no point in moping, when there is still so much to be grateful for. Sure, most people had homes and ovens and lovely cooked food, and less worries than us. But there was no point in comparing apples to oranges. We just had to crack on with what we did have, and focus ahead, instead of what we had right now.

Having the camping kettle and stove was a lifesaver, although it was a pain having to clean the saucepan with only hot water and baby wipes. Still, I could pass the day with a cup of tea in my hand, and even though the UHT milk left bits floating in it, there is just something about having a cuppa that makes everything seem a bit more manageable.

Life's just better with a cuppa.

Where we had parked the car, near the CSA agency, meant people would walk past every day, although it wasn't so obvious, we were there, and we didn't seem to annoy anyone tucked away there. From time to time workers from the agency would say hello, and I was generally up for a chat if they came to the window to check on me. I even started saying hello to the dog walkers that would linger around peering in, they thought they were being subtle – they weren't.

In a naughty way I was hoping one of them might be a lottery winner and take pity on us, but if they were, they never fell for it. Ah well, we can only hope.

I imagined that a few of the houses in the built-up areas nearby often had a topic of conversation around the dinner table, the homeless couple in the car.

I was sitting in the car, as I did everyday debating whether to leave the windows wide open or not because wasps kept flying in and pissing me off while I was trying to write, when I heard footsteps shuffling towards the car.

I rose up to the window thinking it was Ryan – most people didn't get too close, preferring to shout over from the pavement, in case homelessness was contagious. And there was a middle-aged man peering in at me.

'Hello petal, sorry to bother you...'

'That's alright, are you ok?'

'Well,' he laughed. 'That's what I was going to ask you actually, I'm, well, I'm a neighbour.' He said the word like it was in quotation marks, as though he wanted to say 'good Samaritan' but thought better of it.

I looked around comically as though there was another car parked beside me, that I hadn't noticed before.

'I've seen you in the car, I just wanted to see if you were ok?'

He seemed nervous, like he didn't want to put his foot in it and say the wrong thing. He obviously didn't want to come across as nosy or intrusive. He was trying his best, so I smiled at him, hoping it would help settle the battle he was having in his head.

I wanted to tell him the truth. No, I was not ok, not really. I was getting by and surviving. I wondered if he had any idea what that might feel like. I wanted to tell him that I was worried every day. Someone might try to rob us or hurt us – just because that's what people were like sometimes.

I wanted to tell him I felt dirty and subhuman compared to everyone else. I wanted to tell him I was afraid when it was night-time, when cars would pull up and flash their main beam lights into the car. That I was frightened every day that we'd have the police decide enough was enough and take our car away. I wanted to tell him that our very flimsy plan had a very good chance of failing, and there was no back up option. If we wanted to go in a hostel we would be split up, and Ryan would be likelier than me to find his way onto the street, while I – well, I'd be on my own then. A fearful concept that no man could ever truly understand, except for when they think about going to prison.

But I didn't know how to say all that, and if I said it all, it would feel so much more real. So instead I said -

'I'm fine, thank you. This is just a temporary thing.'

'Is there anything I can do? Anything at all?'

We all say that don't we? I've said it countless times to friends going through a hard time. There is never anything you can really do, but we say it anyway. I mean - he could offer a bed for the night, or a shower or a hot dinner. But I could tell he didn't want to go that far. If he did, he'd have offered.

'I don't think so. But thank you.'

'I could get you a phone number for the council. Or- '

'Hello Flower,' Another man appeared, with another floral pet name for me. Seeing that I was talking to someone had obviously caught his eye.

'This is my work colleague' The first guy told me, in lieu of his name.

'So...' The second guy looked into the car. 'You're homeless then.'

This man was abrupt and matter of fact. He had seen his chance to get a good look in and taken it. He wanted to know the gossip.

'Why don't you go to the council?' he smirked as he said it, like he was the first person to not only suggest, but also have knowledge of this option. Almost as though I was stupid for not knowing.

I explained that I'd done that, but we had been classed as intentionally homeless. Then I explained that without an address we weren't eligible for any other help either. It was a catch 22, so we were on our own. But we were finding our way out of it. I sounded defensive, I knew, but he was making me feel that way.

'Well. I hope you're ok. I'd seen you here a few times, but I didn't like to disturb.'

'I'm ok. Thankyou.'

'We get travellers down here, about once a year, I expect you knew that though. We just assumed you were those sorts...' He blathered on, looking around at the rubbish strewn in the hedges.

'They certainly make themselves known, hey John!' He clapped the first man's shoulder to make him acknowledge the previous, untidy tenants.

I didn't want to point out that since staying here I had discovered where all the rubbish was coming from. The people that worked at the CSA would often come to sit in their cars around lunchtime, scoffing sandwiches, chocolate bars and the like. Then they'd empty their cars of all the evidence, and then some – into the bushes next to the car. I'd seen a good handful of them doing it, but of course, the blame lay at the folk who weren't here to defend themselves. Of course, it wouldn't be the civilised people with jobs. Except it was.

'Anyway,' The original man began, seeing where this conversation was going and stepping backwards. 'We will leave you alone, just let us know if you need anything...'

I'll ring you on my bat phone, I thought bitterly. He hadn't left a number or contact. As they strode off to work, I saw the second guy pat Johns back.

'Well done John.' He told him.

Yeah. Fucking well done John.

I sat and sweated out the rest of the day alone.

Chapter 16- The Police, again.

In the evenings, often just before Ryan got back, I had noticed a guy lurking round the gates to the carpark. We'd seen him a few times and I assumed he was a security guard. Black trousers, white shirt on. He had a sinister air about him, which may have been due to him looking a lot like Ian Huntley. I tried to keep an eye on him when I was alone.

He locked up the gates after everyone had left, but recently he had begun to stand around staring straight into the car as the streetlights came on.

I wasn't sure if he was annoyed or if his face just looked like that from so far away, but he was making me feel uncomfortable, and I was about to find out that my gut feeling was exactly right.

Ryan had just got back, and I had the kettle on for his first tea of the day, when we noticed the guy staring into the car again.

'He'd been doing it a lot lately.' I told Ryan, handing him his cup and sitting back with mine.

'If we leave him alone, he'll leave us alone' Ryan said. But I wasn't so sure.

I knew how people felt when they saw us living like this, it was either pity, or hatred. And that guys face wasn't one of pity.

The security guy finished his smoke, walked back to the building and disappeared out of view.

Half an hour later, a white car pulled up directly behind us, blocking us in completely. I couldn't make out the car very well, but I could see the fluorescent yellow on it and knew what it said on it.

POLICE.

'Fuck'.

We wound our seats upright quickly and tidied the dashboard up.

'Hello there!'

The policeman leant into the window. It was a different guy to the last one. I wondered if he had heard about us from the first guy. He had a torch on even though it wasn't fully dark yet. He shone it through the window across our laps and over our feet.

'What are you two up to then?'

'Nothing?' Ryan answered honestly and politely.

I smiled at the policeman. I hoped it looked friendly and not guilty as sin.

'We've just had a cup of tea' I said, like some sort of idiot.

Ryan shot me a look and mouthed 'What the fuck?'

The policeman was still looking in with his torch, he was onto the backseat now. Our manky duvet, the empty Tupperware. Some clothes. A pillow.

'Well, I've had a report of two people in a car, smoking strong cannabis...' He spoke slowly and surely, as though waiting to discover something less than innocuous so he could say the classic – 'Well, well, well...'

Hang on. What?

'Are you sure it's meant about us, sir?' Ryan asked.

'That's what the call said, but I can see- and smell- that you aren't the culprits. False alarm.' He said it brightly. We were off the hook.

'Anyway, as I have been called out, I must run a vehicle check on you, so if I could take your details...?' He tapered off looking at Ryan.

Fake name time. I quickly thought of my best friend Hannah's details. She won't mind. This was the second time in my life a policeman was asking for my details, and the first time I hadn't been able to give her details – because, well, I was with her.

'Oh, I'm Ryan. Ryan Evans. And this is-'

Ok, we are going for real names. Real names it is.

'Gylisa. Potten.' I filled in. Still smiling like a loon.

Ryan gave his date of birth, and everything else he was asked for, and the policeman strode back to his car to put the details into his computer.

'Shit. Shit, shit, shit.'

I knew what was happening, but it felt like slow motion. It felt so agonisingly slow. I knew that he was about to type in the car details, check them against Ryan's name and realise we have no tax, no insurance, even the MOT had run out. And he would have to ask us to step out of the car, and it would be towed away. Crushed most likely, unless we paid some money. But we didn't have money.

It was the law. And police officers' toe that line.

'What are we gonna do Ryan?'

'I don't know. Just go along with it, don't be rude.' He hissed back at me. Still smiling even though the guy wasn't looking anymore.

Ryan could see him typing everything in, frown etched on his head.

Any minute now, we were about to lose it all.

Chapter 17 – The Police (Part Two)

The Policeman got out of his car and walked back up to Ryan's window.

Here we go, I thought. This is rock bottom. We are about to hit it hard.

'Ok, so that's everything checked. Are you sleeping in the car?' He asked.

'Um, yeah. We are. Just for moment, 'til the end of the month.' Ryan stuttered it all out, completely aghast that the guy hadn't cuffed him and yanked him out the car.

'Right, ok. Well, look - good luck, stay out of trouble. Nights are getting colder now...!'

Ryan and I stared at each other. Is that it?

'We will do!' Ryan laughed back. 'Just trying to keep our heads down.'

The policeman nodded and went on his way.

We both breathed a huge sigh of relief.

He wasn't taking the car. Why on earth not?

'Jesus, I was shitting myself that he'd ask to look in here...' He dropped open the glovebox and there was a clear Ziplock bag full of white powder.

'What the fuck is that!?' I gasped. I hadn't seen it before. 'A huge bag of...cocaine?!'

Where the Hell had he got that from? Ryan was laughing now.

'It's not what it looks like, its pre-workout...but I knew that he wouldn't have thought that.'

'I'll bet it is!'

'No really it is, smell it, it's orange flavour.'

I did, and it was.

'If he'd have seen that, he'd have pulled me in straight away, no questions asked. We would have been truly fucked then!'

We laughed at just how close it had been. Fucking pre-workout. I still couldn't believe it.

He had checked the cars details. He must have known we weren't road legal but chose to let it slide. He must have known, but he also must have known that if he reported it, we would *lose* it.

'I can't believe he let us get away with it.'

'I know,' Ryan said. 'He knew we were illegal. What a decent guy.'

'Some things are more important than the law I guess.'

'That or he couldn't be arsed with the paperwork!'

Either way, that had been a close call. Too close. I wondered who thought we'd been smoking weed in the car. I thought about the two old guys I'd spoken to a day before, surely not them?

I looked into the wing mirror and movement caught my eye.

The security guy had been stood in the top carpark the whole time, concealed by the bushes and rapidly falling darkness. He saw me looking, turned and walked off.

Chapter 18 – Sarah.

Ryan had found a newspaper in the van, it was out of date, but I didn't know what was going on in the world as it happened, so it seemed like news to me. I was quietly reading it to pass the time, enjoying an article about a rich porn star being exploited – question mark? When I heard a quiet voice through the window –

'Excuse me?'

I turned to squint at this new interruption. I couldn't see her very well without my contact lenses, but she looked a bit like Sarah Millican. I saw an ID badge around her neck and quickly wondered if she was about to bring more trouble to my car door.

'I don't want to intrude, but I've seen you here for quite a while now. I just wanted to see if you were ok?'

It was the first thing most people asked if they were brave enough to actually talk to me. 'Are you ok?' It's such a strange question to ask someone who is quite obviously not ok, because if I were, I wouldn't be here to be asked. But then again, what do we say?

The first few times it irritated me, Dad always said to me 'Ask a stupid question, get a stupid answer.' And I often considered answering in various rude and idiotic ways. But as the time went on and I could sort out the genuine concern from the nosy parkers. Well, I realised that it really meant 'Do you need someone to talk to?' or 'Can I help you?'

I could see through the blur that the lady in front of me was fighting the same mind battle that John had days before. Not wanting to sound rude, but not sure how else to go about it. She'd clearly been unsure whether to knock on the window at all.

'I...I don't want to bother you, but I wanted to know if there was anything I could do?'

Her words reminded me of the note I found weeks earlier. I still wondered if that was a genuine response, or if it had had sinister undertones. Was the mysterious Matt being a good Samaritan, or was I an easy target? I'll never know.

I started with the usual 'This is only temporary, we are waiting for Ryan's wages to come through, no I'm not on my own...Yes we have tried the council...'

But her expression was so sympathetic that I couldn't keep everything from tumbling out. The filter just fell away and before I knew it, I was telling her about Dad, and being bullied at work, and being afraid of everything, but also being so afraid it would all stay the same. Before I knew it, she was wiping away a tear.

'I'm sorry, I didn't mean to upset you...' I told her, feeling foolish.

I forget, quite often that not everyone has the same experiences as each other. For some of us, life can be hard and uncomfortable and sad.

For others, life comes easy, and bad things are just something that happens in the news, and they find themselves rubbernecking at accidents, because they've never found themselves so close to something so tragic.

Except for those of us that it does happen to and we realise that these things do happen and there is no 'how am I going to survive this?' you just do. You just do.

And it's hard and horrible and it puts all the silly first world problems into perspective. Then you tell someone who doesn't get it and you see how this would affect a 'normal' person, and you realise that whatever you are going through is not normal – but you still have to survive it, and keep on going.

A lot of people mistake survival as 'strength' and will tell you 'If you hadn't gone through that you wouldn't be as strong as you are now.' But I've realised that that is bullshit.

We don't become strong, we become resilient. It is simply an act of survival, and we are unlucky enough to need to get through it. Many people don't.

No. Being strong isn't a virtue. It isn't a compliment either. It is too often a necessity.

The lady asked me about my family and friends, and whether they had tried to offer any help or if they knew where I was. I told her truthfully, they don't know. And we don't want them to know because we would have to admit that we had failed. And how could we ask for help? We didn't want to burden anyone else with this situation, we just wanted to keep our heads down and push through it.

Its temporary. I reminded her. She didn't seem so sure.

'They would help if they knew.' She told me.

Her faith in other humans was so humbling, and so naïve it made me feel sad.

'My name is Sarah. I work in the nursery just in front of the CSA.' She pointed the building out to me.

'If you need anything, come in there and ask for me. Once the kids have all gone home, I'm in there for an hour or two, and there is a shower and leftover food from lunch. I can box it up for you both, you are welcome to it. Anything that can help...'

Once again, I was speechless. It didn't feel real that someone could offer and be so pure in their intentions. It was hard to believe and even harder to accept.

'Thank you, Sarah. I'm Gylisa. And I really appreciate the offer.'

She reiterated it to me one more time, perhaps reading on my face that I had no intention of turning up because it felt so rude. I was grateful. Truly. But how could I turn up and accept her charity?

She promised me that if I asked for her at the security gate, I would be let in. It was up to me. She had to go back in then, she'd used her entire lunchbreak speaking to me. Before she left, I thanked her again, feeling like the word wasn't powerful enough to convey how I really felt at the sincere act of kindness.

Now she'd gone, I felt strange. Her pity reminded me that this was an awful situation. It was easier to just keep those feelings at bay, just let the minutes turn into hours and look forward – reminding ourselves that this was all going to be over soon.

The emotions it left with me were always harder to avoid at night. The cold would creep in from under our seats at first, inching under the duvet and reminding us that we weren't warm and safe, not really.

Dads house had always been cold, I'd wake up most mornings in the winter with the windows frosted over and able to see my breath. When it got cold in the car, I'd shut my eyes and pretend I was there, although it didn't make me feel safe – it made me feel that I was somewhere else. Like nothing had changed.

Now Sarah had inadvertently forced me to remember that there was a whole world of people out there, with their own lives and their own troubles and it was still weird for us to be doing this. It wasn't normal. I had been so wrapped up in the abnormality of it that I hadn't for a second reminded myself that living out of a car is not a normal turn of events. It is not some rite of passage that regular folk must go through before being granted an average life with 2.5 kids and a driveway.

Sarah had also said if we found ourselves in any trouble to go and find her as well. It reminded me that we were hanging by a thread. The police could take the car away. We could be robbed- although I had rationalised that one to myself – I figured that no one would rob us because the car wasn't worth anything and they'd have to deal with all our belongings. Robbing us would just mean having to do a bloody tip run.

My other ever-increasing fear was about something happening to Ryan. I'd have no idea if he had an accident at work, or even on his way back to the car. No one knew he was living here; no one would even know who to call. I worried every minute past his usual 'home-time' that he wouldn't turn up, and I'd be left to face this all alone, no idea where he was or what might have happened to him.

His work was our only safety, and it felt like it was made from spiders' silk.

But now, there was Sarah. If I needed someone to help, I could try her. I pushed that thought down again.

This was temporary, I reminded myself. Nothing bad is going to happen.

Chapter 19 – Bank Holiday.

After the workers had gone home from the CSA, and the security guy had packed up and left himself, the last dog walkers made their way home for dinner – the layby we were parked in became peaceful, and quiet. The first few nights the noise from the main road nearby had been annoying, but now I found it soothed me, breaking up the eerie silences with an occasional amniotic whoosh.

It wasn't like that every evening though, and too often a car would pull up nearby. We were never sure if they were here to gawp at us, or if they'd pulled up for something else. Some parked, saw us and swiftly left. Others would hang around and we'd peek at them through the sun visor mirrors.

'Who do you think they are?' Ryan would whisper.

'Doggers.' I would say, every time.

'Not again.'

'Definitely, look at the state of 'em.'

I'd reach up to flick on the door light and Ryan would fight my arm down.

'Don't give them the signal!' He'd wrestle with me.

'I'm not! You are!'

Mostly, we would shit ourselves that it was the police again, called to our attention because someone had got ticked off with our being there again. For the first time I felt for gypsies and travellers – we were trying to stay out the way, but where else were we meant to go?

One night, after darkness, I was staring idly out the window with my head pressed right up against the glass. It was getting cold the moment the sun disappeared, so I had the duvet wrapped around me, totally zoned out.

A young couple walked out the alley and saw me, neither realising that I was a real person. I must have looked like a hairdresser's practise head or something, because they jumped out their skin.

'That is fucking weird!' They screeched.

I stayed stock still, waiting for them to get closer so I could make eye contact with them and really freak them out, but they scarpered!

Next to the Tesco roundabout a couple of hundred yards from us, there was a Domino's pizza being built. The construction brought a lot more people down our hidden little road, where it had usually been deserted in the evening. So, until around 11pm, there were cars coming and going.

As it got closer to that time, the cars coming and going seemed to get swept up in a weird witching hour. Before then we were generally left well alone.

Past 9.30pm, we were fair game. Boy racer cars would turn up and flash their main beams into the car, they'd honk and shout at us. On two occasions two cars parked behind and beside us, blocking us in completely. They thought it was fun, but for us it was horrible.

Every Friday, a moped crew would whizz in and whoop with delight that we were still there. They found our set up deeply amusing and would yell and laugh right up against the windows. One of them threw a can at the car, they tore off a towel I'd accidentally left on the roof and threw it into the bushes. They'd even bang on the roof if they couldn't see us. I'm sure if I had been alone, they'd have acted much worse. We just tried to ignore them, although I did flick them the bird a few times. That made them act worse. Something to do before they headed home to their Mums house.

One evening Ryan said enough was enough and we drove up onto Dartmoor for the night.

'About time we had a proper night of peace'

Well, we were wrong about that. While it was amazing to sleep without the towels on the windows – there were no streetlights up there, in fact there was no light pollution at all, even though we were only a stone's throw away from our lay-by. It was pitch black, so we could see every star, every constellation. It was breathtakingly beautiful.

But all throughout the night there was a heavy shuffling and thumping all around the car. It sounded like someone huge was walking in circles around the car, trying to look in! I haven't been scared of monsters for a long time, but I was too scared to even whisper to Ryan about it. I'd heard of the Beast of Bodmin Moor but surely it wasn't real?

Something outside sighed loudly and I froze with fear. Then the thing let off a soft whinny and I relaxed instantly. Of course!

'It's the wild ponies!'

Ryan leant forward to flick the car lights on, and there surrounding the car were several wild ponies, huddling together, unsure what to make of this car on their land. We chuckled to each other, relaxed and drifted off to sleep.

In the morning, I let the ponies lick sugar off the dashboard, which was another regrettable decision because they left green drool all over it. I was retching while I squirted my anti-bacterial hand gel over it and wet wiped it clean again. The ponies stank as well, but that made two of us, I guess.

I'd have stayed up there every night if we could, but there were a lot of signs saying otherwise and we didn't want to have another police episode. After that night, strangely, the yobs stopped visiting for a week or two, and I wondered if they'd turned up that night to discover the empty space. Maybe it had humanized us, or perhaps they thought we'd left because of them. Either way, it was nice to be back somewhere sort of familiar without the banging on the roof.

****

I thought about Sarah's offer a lot. I was desperate for another shower and we couldn't justify the cost yet – not until we were a bit closer to the end of the month again. I'd step out the car some days and walk along the pavement, peering into the trees that hid the building I presumed she worked in. Every time I'd stand opposite and go to walk over before feeling silly and heading back to the car. I'd mull it over in my head again for an hour, and the process would repeat. I just couldn't go over there, she was being polite, I'd tell myself.

I'll go over there and she'll be on her day off, and then I'll be forcibly removed. I catastrophised. Banned from the premises. I'd walk the pavement again, squint over and then find myself back in the car.

Maybe she'd forgotten anyway.

Friday rolled around once more, although I have long since stopped logging the date in my diary. I sat flicking through it, pen in hand when there was another delicate tap on the window.

'Hello again...'

It was Sarah. She hadn't forgotten me.

I was genuinely pleased to see her and dived to wind down the window and say hello, smiling widely. We said our hellos and she said she knew I hadn't been to the nursery, but it was ok.

'I just wanted to let you know that it'll be closed on Monday, its bank holiday...'

'Ok...'

She held up a huge cool bag from Tesco.

'And I don't know about you, but I always like a treat on the bank holiday. And I couldn't bear the thought of you two being here on your own, so – I got you some things...'

I stared at her open mouthed. She didn't need to do this.

'Don't be offended, I just guessed what things you might like or need.'

I stuttered over my words trying to thank her, I just couldn't find the right sentence and my stomach felt heavy with emotion. I didn't want to cry and make her feel uncomfortable, so I swallowed my words and hoped it shone out of my face. I just couldn't comprehend such a generous act of kindness. It was above and beyond anything I'd experienced, in this life or the previous.

We chatted for another 15 minutes or so, I'd have spoken to her for hours if it was what she wanted, I just had no idea how to repay the kindness. I swore to myself that when we were back on our feet, I'd find her again, and thank her. Properly. I'd treat her next time.

I didn't know when would be considered the polite amount of time since she left before diving into the bag, and I considered waiting for Ryan – but that was another five hours away and it was sat there on the back seat just asking to be opened. I dived in.

There was all sorts in there. Crisps, chocolate, bottles of squash, tea bags, jam tarts, croissants – Tesco's finest. That touched me even more, that she'd made the real effort to make it special for us. There were sweets, fruit, fresh bread, and a TESCO gift card for £20.

I cried then and I didn't care. My own Dad wouldn't do this for us. It wasn't about the money or the actual stuff but the act itself. Never in my life had I met someone who was so overwhelmingly GOOD. She'd done this with no ulterior motive, no need for recognition. Just because she wanted to help, and this was how she chose to do it. I cried for the first time in weeks. About everything, about my old job, living with Dad, being hungry, Ryan working so hard, every little unfair act before this.

Then, when I had finally run out of tears, I even did a tester check – imagining Ryan and I's funerals. But I was done. I took out one croissant and a juice and bundled everything else back in for Ryan's surprise when he got back.

He spotted the bag the moment he got in, and I excitedly pulled it out to show him.

'Where did you get all this?' He asked me, accusingly.

'I didn't buy it!' wrongly assuming he thought I'd wasted the rest of our money rations on treats. 'The nursery lady – Sarah – she dropped it off.'

He eyed me suspiciously. This was not the reaction I had imagined.

'She said its bank holiday and she wanted us to have some treats. So, she got it all...have a look!'

I wanted him to feel as touched and excited as I had. I wanted it to be a good thing. Something to be grateful for, something to break up the miserable day.

'No, she got it for you. She doesn't even know me.' He huffed jealously. I bit back my first response.

'It's not like I asked for it, Ryan, would you have preferred I told her to take it away?'

'I suppose you've eaten half of it all then...'He said spitefully. I ignored him.

He grumbled about being tired and stressed but peered in the bag anyway. He took a chocolate bar out and I busied myself with making a hot drink for us both. He probably *was* tired and stressed, I knew his days were long and hard, but I wasn't trying to be annoying, I was trying to make him happy. And I had very little to work with. I strained his teabag so hard the spoon bent.

Misery is like a vicious cycle, one person is miserable, so they take it out on another, only it doesn't dissipate like that, it just makes two people miserable. Then the second person takes it out on something else, like an innocent teaspoon, and then what – two miserable, homeless fuckers and a spoon you can't even eat with anymore.

Ryan was getting grumpier and grumpier lately, not that I couldn't see why. But it did make me feel on edge. I hadn't seen this side to Ryan before, ever. He was a sunshine person, like me. Only now it was like that light was dimming, and I didn't know how much longer he could take like this. He sipped his tea.

'That tastes rank.'

I closed my eyes. I knew the tea bags were crap, but we couldn't afford any others. Same with the milk, we couldn't have fresh and I tried to keep the UHT stuff cool by storing it under the car and out of the heat – but there wasn't much more I could do.

'Sorry love.'

Why was I saying sorry? I wasn't sorry. I sounded weak and pathetic. I didn't want an argument, although I could think of plenty of things to say that would start one. I sighed instead.

'What are you fucking sighing for now?'

'Just thinking about stuff, that's all.'

'Look, if you're so unhappy, then go home. I've told you already. Go back to your mums.'

I stared at him.

'Are you joking?'

Is this really what he thought this was all about? I wasn't unhappy with the situation, I was getting through it, and with a smile on my face most days – which was more than could be said for him. The miserable prick.

I wasn't staying here for the fun of it, I was staying here because we were in this together. I didn't want to leave him. If he couldn't see that, then I might as well bugger off.

'I don't want to go home.' I said it sharply, with no room for question. I'm not weak, so I don't want to sound that way.

'Well I wish you would. I hate seeing you here, living like this. It's not what you deserve.'

'What?' I had been ready for a full-blown argument; I was practically making the 'fuh' sound ready to tell him to 'Fuh-ck Right Off.' My heart softened instantly. He wasn't annoyed with me; he was annoyed with himself.

'I'm sorry, alright? I'm sorry that I'm not good enough, and I'm not doing enough.' It spilled out quickly, every thought he'd been holding in for the last two months.

When he finished, he looked out the window, avoiding my gaze.

So that's what he thinks. He thinks this is all down to him, while I sit here day in day out thinking it's all down to me.

I reached over and settled my hand on his thigh.

'Ryan, we are in this together. I don't want to leave you behind. That would make me unhappy! I want to get through this together. I need you. You need me.'

He looked at me, then laid his hand over mine.

'It's not forever. We will laugh about this one day.' I smiled at him, hoping for a mirrored response.

'What if it is? What if we don't get the flat? What if I lose my job? What if we lose the car?!' He was irritated by the loss of control on the situation now.

We hadn't discussed this, not properly. Discussing it made it real, and making it real meant it could happen. I didn't want to think about it, and I knew he didn't either. Of course, it was all either of us thought about once we'd gone quiet at night. What will happen? What if we break through the spider web net?

'It's not going to happen Ryan; we have to think positively. It'll work out.'

'You don't know that, so don't start your think positive bullshit with me. We need to think about this stuff?!'

Well, we argued then.

I let rip. I yelled, he yelled. I called him an idiot. He said I was living with my head in the clouds. Maybe I was. But it beat spending my time worrying or being a miserable cunt. I got out the car.

'Run to your mother!' He shouted back at me. I stalked off further. He called after me, asking me where I was going.

And then telling me not to disappear. He carried on calling after me until I was out of earshot. But he didn't follow.

I hated him. I hated the car. I hated this street, and the lights that turned off at 2am. It scared me every time, I was always awake. I hated this situation, and all the ones leading up to it. I hated the security guard from the carpark opposite. I just hated everything. I couldn't even cry because I'd emptied my tears out earlier. Fucking crying.

I walked a bit further before realising I had no idea where to go. I didn't want to be near people, so Tesco was out. I hadn't gone the right direction for the woodland, or the fairy meadow. And I wasn't walking past Ryan again now. I wanted him to worry a bit. Serve him right for moaning about my tea making. Arsehole.

I sat on the pavement and looked at the dirt in the gutter. A shard of glass caught my eye.

I turned it over and admired its sharp edges. I briefly considered stabbing myself with it, for something to do. Sympathy from Ryan for bleeding, followed by apologies for making me do such a thing.

You manipulative little witch, I thought. I threw the shard back down. I'd probably get tetanus or something and die, which would be annoying, and a tad melodramatic considering this is the first argument Ryan and I had ever had.

We needed each other.

Didn't we?

I let myself consider the opposite. If Ryan and I went our separate ways now, what would I do? No job? No money. Nowhere to really go to. I'd have to beg for a place at the Hostel I suppose. On my own. Then take the steps from there. The bottom rung of society. Whereas Ryan- well, without me the tenancy fees would be cheaper, so he'd do that. Live in the car until he secured the flat, then – well, he'd have a roof over his head, a job, and only one person to provide for.

I needed Ryan. But he didn't need me at all.

I considered what I really would do, what options I truly had. I drew a blank. Maybe I could call the number from Matts note. At least if he was a killer my plight would soon be over with.

I went back to the car.

Chapter 20 – The Day Mum Didn't Come.

We stuffed our faces that weekend, fuck the rations!

After said our apologies and hugged it out, we drove up to the moors for the next three nights and stroked the ponies. We walked through the bracken and looked at the stunning views. The landscape up there was like nothing I'd seen before, it was like another planet, and it seemed so untouched until we came across the old engine houses dotted across the moors, or 'danger – flooded mine' signs.

Don't get me wrong, I love the seaside, and the quaint towns and everything that came with them but being amongst nature in the countryside was where I felt happiest. The air felt clearer, there wasn't anyone around to bother us. It was perfect.

We stocked up on water and more essentials with some on the money on the Tesco gift card and used the rest for petrol. Then we drank copious amounts of tea and pissed amongst nature. I wasn't sure if freedom really existed, but this was as close as we could get.

I dreamed of a little house on the moors, with thick blankets and a cosy fireplace to drink tea around. We'd get there in the end, I thought. I could sense it. Maybe not now, but one day. One day we'd have it all.

Ryan kept interrupting my daydreams with apologies about where we were and what we were doing.

I told him over and over, it was never what he could give me, but who he was. That's what I needed. The material things didn't bother me in the slightest, I'd get by with nothing if I had to. This was just the low part of the adventure, that's all. What's a protagonist without a few hiccups along the way?

On Sunday evening, during another tea and talking session, a text pinged through. We both jumped to the phone, although usually it was a reminder of how much debt we were in. 'You are in arrears with your bill, despite several reminders. Bailiffs will take action soon.'

Bailiffs, if they ever found us, would take one look at the car and scoff at it. It would cost them more to get rid of it than it would to get any money out of us!

But this time it wasn't from our mobile provider, it was my mum!

'I'm coming to Plymouth on Thursday.' That was all it said. No exact time, no 'where shall we meet?'

It didn't matter, excitement rippled through me.

My mum was coming.

My mum.

My MUM.

I didn't question it, I was too excited to see her, my MUM. I felt giddy, would she really come here? Would she!?

'Can't wait to see you! What time?!' I texted her back instantly.

'After work. Love you.'

My mum!

I looked at Ryan, and showed him the texts, beaming with joy. He nodded.

'I think it's time we stopped by Nanny and Grandad's.'

Ryan's grandparents lived in Bodmin, we'd seen them a couple of times before living in the car, and they'd welcomed us to stay with them, but as Ryan's Nanny was having treatment for breast cancer we didn't want to impose, at all. So, we'd kept quiet about it.

Now we were thinking about cashing in – one weekend stay please. We looked at the dates on the calendar. One week away was pay day. Finally, *the end of the month.*

What a way to celebrate the end of this awful luck - with a proper night's stay in a house!? A taster night back in normality, before we would return to it ourselves. And anyway, Ryan reasoned – we can have tidy up of ourselves and the car before we see the estate agents again. A good point.

****

That week couldn't have gone by any slower. Every day I was aching for the evening to come so I was one more sleep closer to seeing my mum. The excitement was palpable. I felt like it was a sign, mum was going to be here! I could hug her, talk to her, enjoy her company. It felt like years had passed since we'd done that. There was no greater comfort than that of my mum.

We would laugh about all this stuff; it was a blip! We'd have fish and chips and go to a beach. We'd finally get back to enjoying Cornwall for what it was.

I found myself awake most the nights and sleeping away the days, so desperate I was for the time to pass.

Until finally, the day was here – Thursday.

Mum hadn't text, not the night before nor all morning, and I watched the phone like a hawk. I didn't dare touch it in case the battery died, so I'd sit and wait and watch the road behind. I don't know why but I felt like mum would just 'know' where we were, that's what mums do. They just know. It's part of their Mum Magic.

A few hours passed, and no contact. I wondered if she was driving yet, mentally calculating how long it would take her, what time she'd arrive if she set off now.

Or now.

Or now.

I waited and waited, but the phone didn't ring. No texts came through.

Mum's done this before, I told myself, remembering times my brother and I would be stood outside our primary school, after all the cars had gone but the caretakers and the last few teachers. We'd wait 'til the streetlights came on and huddle together. Tom always reassured me 'We could just walk home...' It was only 6 miles away. Then it happened when we moved to Hampshire, and we didn't know the way home at all. It had happened even while I was at college, waiting for mum to come and meet me, waiting past 4pm, until 6pm rolled around and her car would finally trundle up.

'I'm sorry!' She'd call, and we'd jump in, grateful to see her and half-secure that she did always turn up eventually.

I walked along the pavement all the way up to the roundabout, more for something to do than something proactive. I took the phone in case it ran out of signal, or she rang while I was waiting.

I watched every car intently, trying to see if mum was in one. I knew what car she had but it didn't stop me looking in every single one. My mum is always doing favours or having them returned so would often turn up in someone else's car for God knows what reason. Usually because her old bangers would have bit the dust, just as she needed it to be reliable.

Maybe that was what was making her late? The car?! I felt a fool for not thinking it earlier. She'd probably faffing with the car, that's why she hasn't text. I didn't want to be like my sister and hound her into a stress, so I just waited.

And waited.

And waited.

Ryan got back. Expecting to see mum with me he asked, 'Oh, where is she then?'

I didn't know. The late afternoon turned into evening, and then into the night.

'Maybe she'll text tomorrow, before she leaves?' he suggested.

'Yeah, maybe.' I watched leaves fall from the trees and didn't say much else.

*****

Friday came. No word from Mum. I couldn't ring her, although I was tempted to try on the payphone in Tesco, but I didn't know how much it would cost.

Lunchtime rolled around, and I finished the last stale croissant and gulped down a tea. I walked up to the roundabout again and sat on the verge. And then I waited some more.

4pm, no sign of mum.

7pm, I spotted Ryan's figure making his way back to car, I ran to greet him.

'Still no mum then?'

I shook my head. He wrapped an arm around me, and we headed back to the car together.

At 10pm, I stopped looking for headlights, and a text finally came through.

'Sorry G. Will come next week instead. Phones been off. X X X X X X X X X X'

Chapter 21- The Day She Did.

I felt miserable all weekend after that, Ryan tried to cheer me up – but I didn't even want to walk around Tesco and choose all the things we'd need for our imaginary new flat. I half-heartedly stroked some towels and then moped back to the car.

Truth was, mum not turning up made me feel like everything that I had been excited about wasn't going to happen, especially because I had wanted it to so badly and yet I'd gotten it so wrong.

I wasn't going to hold my breath for Mum's next visit. Ryan arranged a weekend at his grandparent's house for the next week anyway, so we'd have something to look forward to.

We wandered around the fairy meadow instead, walking through to the little village nearby. Ryan splashed out and bought some cookies, so we took them back to go with a nice stale UHT tea.

As we got back to the car Ryan's phone starting buzzing.

G's Mum.

I didn't know if I wanted to answer to hear more excuses about last week again. But then again if I changed my mind, I couldn't ring her back.

I answered.

She kept up her usual jolly façade, telling me that she was definitely coming this time, and she'd bring Brad, and my brother, Tom with her. I couldn't stay miserable with her then, she seemed genuinely excited to see us, so it didn't matter that she'd bailed on us before... I wanted to see my mum!

She told me she would come on Friday, and I told her we were viewing a flat on Saturday, and that Ryan's grandparents had said we could stay there, but this weekend they were away – so we'd have the house to ourselves. It worked out well, as everyone would have a bed to sleep in. That was the better news for Ryan and me - it had been well over three months since we'd slept in a proper bed, and Ryan was starting to groan whenever he uncurled himself out of the car.

I tried not to count down the days this time, not allowing myself to be excited until I physically saw her car with her in it.

Friday came and I had something other than waiting for mum to be getting on with.

It was payday.

There should be two months of wages in the bank, plenty to pay our rent, deposit and agency fees, as well as enjoy the weekend ahead, within reason. I don't think we'd have been able to waste money even if we had it to spare!

I couldn't help but tremble with nerves as I slid the card into the ATM once more. I didn't want to imagine what I'd do if I had to tell Ryan there was nothing in there again, I'd probably just take myself off somewhere to die – like elephants do.

I put in the numbers and the machine whirred, ready to hand over Ryan's very, very hard-earned cash.

I peered at the screen, ready to see a comma, for the first time in nearly four months.

Available Balance: £840.

My heart dropped into my shoes.

That wasn't right. It wasn't enough.

Not again.

We needed at least £960, just to be given the keys. Never mind surviving for another month. Plus, petrol to work.

And the car. What were we going to do? Why wasn't there more in there? I knew Ryan had worked the days; I knew because I had seen him go. He'd come back every day, dirty and tired. Stressed and exhausted. This wasn't *fair*.

Life isn't fair, Gylisa.

I took out his card, and leant against the wall, with my eyes closed tight. How was I going to tell Ryan?

Another month, we would have to wait another month, in this god forsaken car, Ryan doing his ridiculous job – and for what? A pittance?! How were we ever going to get out of this *fucking mess.*

I sat and I worried until 6pm. The phone rang and it startled me. *Mum.* Of course, I hadn't given that a scrap of thought since I'd seen those numbers on the screen. *Mum was coming.*

'Are you near a Tesco?'

She was here! My worrying would have to wait, mum had finally driven all this way to see me! To see us...! My heart rose again, all was not lost, because mum was here. She would know what to do. I hoped.

I gave her directions to the roundabout and told her I'd wait there so she'd see me.

Then I legged it over there, squinting at every car going past, then there she was, waving madly in the driver's seat, Brad smiling in the other. And my brother, stood up with his head and shoulders through the sunroof, pointing at a huge tray of pink doughnuts they'd obviously bought on the way.

The other drivers on the road must have thought I was having a seizure I was waving so wildly and excitedly. They had come to find me, and here they were.

I pointed them towards our tiny car park, with our little car parked right into the corner, and mum swung her car next door.

'Neighbours!' She laughed, not missing a beat.

They all stretched as they got out the car and I hugged them all, I was beyond happy to see them. Something so familiar in our strange setting, it was like realising you were in a dream and something strange was happening, but not being able to wake up.

I flung the car door open and pointed in.

'Would you like a grand tour?' I asked.

I pointed to the dirty footwell, with the battered kettle and stove. 'Kitchen.'

Then I pointed above it to the dashboard. 'Dining area.'

I pointed to my seat. 'And the bedroom!'

They laughed.

It was music to my ears.

We laughed all the time, at things that just didn't happen in other families. Like the time Dads car handles wouldn't unlock because it was a frosty morning, and he got so angry he threw a log at the car and dented it. My grandma had commented 'I don't think that's a very wise thing to do, what would you do if it were a person not letting you into somewhere else?'

'Grandma, I think Dad would throw a log at them too.' I'd said, and grandma pursed her lips while we all sniggered about it.

We laughed at Dads hypo's when they got scary, as though it was all a silly act, just laugh it off and we will make him better in a moment. We laughed when Dad threw Mums things out, as they smashed on the ground, telling him 'Well, she didn't like that clock that much, anyway.'

I still laugh at things now, although I know when to deal with it properly instead. But life is better when you are laughing, and so laugh at the tiny car-come-house we did.

I was so glad they'd came.

Mum threw her car door open too, revealing the mess inside. Honestly if you'd had to pick which car belonged to the homeless couple, you'd never have chosen ours.

She found what she was looking for and wielded it to us. A camping stove, and large kettle.

'Kettle on then!' She smiled.

Brad began to busy himself with setting it all up, he likes to be busy like that, while mum does all the yapping. Tom offered the doughnuts he was holding around again, while Mum chatted away about God knows what. Mine and Ryan's quiet corner had been well and truly taken over.

Mum was rolling three cigarettes now, and people from the CSA were beginning to stare. She looked back over our newly taken over camp and knocked my arm.

'Hey look, we are the jippos! Jiiiipppppooooos!' She sang it loud and proud, jigging around, two half rolled cigarettes in her hand.

Ah well, I half cringed, half shrugged, laughing at her. If the coppers turned up later – we would be far away in Bodmin, hopefully acting a little bit more civilised.

It amused me how we all fell into easy conversation, drinking tea and smoking, 'catching up' The same way any other families would, except instead of the setting being a lovely garden centre with cream teas in front of us, it was two battered old cars with two camping stoves in the middle, all of us sat with a car door open as we had no proper chairs. It was quite amusing.

As we chatted away, Mum looked over my shoulder and began waving wildly again.

After all this noise and chaos, I'd forgotten all about Ryan finishing work soon. Which reminded me of something else. I'd have to tell him about the money. Again. My stomach dipped unpleasantly.

Brad made him a tea, and Tom offered him a doughnut while Mum got in his face about this and that and the other. I could see Ryan was feeling overwhelmed, and he needed a minute to adjust, so the moment he drank his tea – we got in our respective cars, ready to convoy to his Nanny's house.

He jammed the keys in the ignition, but the car didn't start. It juddered for a second, before dying completely.

Ryan looked at me knowingly. The car had been a bit jittery for a few days now, and Ryan had repeatedly told me not to leave the car doors open, because the door lights came on, and the battery would run flat. And now it had. I'd only had them open a few times, to let the breeze in, or while I was tidying up. Sometimes I needed the light on in the night so I could read or write, or to find my way after having a nature wee.

'Have you got any car leads Mum?' I shouted over Ryan's side.

'No!'

'Feck.'

Ryan's mood was turning sour, and I still hadn't had the chance to tell him about the money. It was the last thing I wanted to do; this was meant to be our last weekend!

'I'll ring my boss.' He borrowed Mums phone and called Lee, who said it was no trouble! He'd swing down right away and get us sorted. The trouble was it meant he'd see the car for the first time and realise exactly how we'd been living. Like I said before, some people just can't imagine things until they are right in front of them. And this was going to be a shock.

'On the bright side – when we get the flat, I'll be allowed to take a van home, so we can fuck this car right off.' Ryan shrugged, content at least that this was our last weekend like this.

I murmured back.

Oh god, I needed to tell him.

'I checked the bank today actually; I need to talk to you about that…'

'Oh god. What now?' He stopped fiddling with the car and looked at me.

'There was only £840 in there.'

'What?! Why so little?'

'I don't know?!' I shrugged; my guess was as good as his. I help my hands up. He fumed some more, but it wasn't for me to know, this was his job.

'Ask Lee when he turns up.'

'For fucks sake, that's it then. In the car, another month…' He threw himself back into the car and put his head in his hands.

Mum poked her head in my side.

'What's up Ryan-lion?' She said in a sing-song voice.

'Nothing,' he said flatly. 'I'm just tired.'

'He didn't get paid as much as we thought he would. So, we aren't sure if we can get the flat this weekend now.'

Ryan shot me a dirty look for spilling the secret. But like I said, I don't like lying.

'Oh, I know how you feel mate, work all month – get paid fuck all! Welcome to the club!'

I'm sure she didn't mean it to sound so horrendously patronising, like Ryan was stupid for not knowing that's how adult life worked. It would just restart every month like some kind of fucked up Groundhog Day. There was no escaping this.

To Ryan's credit, he didn't say a word. Just shot a dirty look at her back instead.

****

Lee came, got his jump leads out of the car and began sorting it. He was a nice lad, didn't bat an eye at the situation that met him.

'Just try the keys again mate!' He called to Ryan, who did so.

The car jumped into life. Nothing more needed to be done. If nothing else, we had the weekend ahead to think of our plan. For now, destination: Bodmin.

Chapter 22 - The True Beginning.

We settled in quickly, everything seemed like such a novelty. Television, sofas, space to move around in! The tiny bungalow was a mansion to us. We had showers and Ryan bought some fish and chips. We gorged ourselves, and Ryan and I fell into the super-king bed. I want to say we fell asleep in an instant, but we both found it was too much room, too flat, too soft and too comfortable!

We finally fell asleep, for the first time with so much space to ourselves it felt like we were at opposite ends of the house.

In the morning, I rang the estate agents while everyone faffed around, to arrange another viewing for later that day. I knew we'd seen the flat, but I was desperate to see it again, to get a feel for it. To see if it really would be mine.

I'd planned it over and over in my head, no matter how many times Ryan reminded me that it'd probably be gone by now, it was the first place I thought of when we walked around Tesco picking out kitchen bins and bedding. I had hand-drawn floor plans from memory and guessed where everything that we didn't own yet, would go. It was going to be ours, I told Ryan. I just know it.

When we viewed it before, the estate agent had told us it was popular, so wouldn't stay vacant for long. I'd assumed it was a sales tactics, but it still worried us. Now it had been months since and it was still available. Ha! I thought, I knew she'd lied.

I thought about it all day, crossing my fingers, wishing when I saw the clock on 11:11. Whispering it under my breath, telling myself over and over, this is going to happen. I can feel it.

Ryan was the realist. He'd say 'I know you want it but how are we going to afford it? We don't have enough money. You can't just wish that bit away.'

I could, and I would.

Two hours later, we were sat by the river in Looe, lovely Looe, where we had first arrived in Cornwall all those weeks ago. It felt like we had come full circle.

The car had simply been a blip. Mum cooked a fry up for us all. It was the most food we'd eaten in months!

'Beats eating fucking soup!' I nudged Ryan. Although we will be back on that diet on Monday. Funny really, that for so many people 'the diet starts Monday' is a decision, restricting food is a lifestyle choice, but for us it was a necessity. I hadn't thought about my body image at all for weeks, and I'd hardly noticed. Mum had commented how thin we were looking, instead of that feeling like a compliment – it felt like it was proof of our failures. Survival looked thin, but I wanted to feel strong again.

Best make the most of it, I figured – and helped myself to another sausage.

We all fell quiet after breakfast, full and enjoying the late morning sun. Brad opened the car and a Tesco bag flew out. My mind went back to the bag that Sarah gave us. I felt guilty that I hadn't let her know we were going. I didn't want her to worry, or think I was rude for disappearing without a trace. She might have noticed the empty spaces today, if she was working. And here I was having a great time while she probably scanned the Plymouth Herald for any news of us. I added it to my mental list of things to worry about later though, as Mum, Brad and Tom wanted to walk around Looe for a bit, while Ryan and I had to go and see a man about a flat.

Getting back into our car I realised how grimy it all was. I didn't notice so much when it was all I was used to, but now I'd been in a clean house, and a clean bed and had a shower – I felt greasy and dirty just sitting in here.

'Maybe we shouldn't park outside the flat.' I told Ryan, wrinkling my nose with a smile.

****

We met with the estate agent, the young guy from before, who was even more jittery and skittish than last time. He dropped the keys trying to shake them into the door, and had to disappear to fetch another pair before we were allowed in.

Ryan and I hung around awkwardly for a moment, this time getting a proper look at the shop opposite. 'Annie's Attic' read the sign, although it was peeling, and sun bleached.

In the midlands, Antiques shops are well presented, laid out so you can have a good walk around, sit on a chair or two. There's even one with a café in it, so you can have a cream tea while you ponder what old crap you'd like to buy. Ryan and I had visited it often, killing time away from home. That was, until one afternoon the dust had seemed to give me the farts, and I'd loudly trumped at an old man sitting with his wife. I'd dived into the old fur coats hissing at Ryan to 'take the blame!' But he'd scarpered to leave me to face up to my sins.

This shop was nothing like that. It looked like a hoarder's house, but with a glass front. There was only just enough space to step into the shop door, shuffle around in a circle to have a look at the piles of junk, and then step back out. One fart would knock the place down, by the looks of it.

As we stood there, someone wanted to have a look at something out of reach from the shop door. A thin, blonde, older woman with a cigarette in her mouth hobbled over and grabbed a litter picking tool. She leant over to 'pick' the item, and hand it over to the man asking to see it.

'I'm asking twelve, but you can have it for ten.' She said, a loud Cornish accent drawling out from her tiny frame. The man pondered this deal, turning the item over in his hands.

We stepped closer to the window to have a good look.

A tiny gold compact mirror caught our eyes at the same time. I loved antique-y things, and anything vintage. The woman spotted us and came over.

'You interested?' She asked, following our line of sight to the compact. 'Ahh, yes lovely piece tha' is.'

I shook my head, but she was already leaning in, dangerously close to knocking all the brightly colour glass vases, clocks and other fragile bits over. She took out some books and a whole load of things crashed down out of sight, but she wasn't the least bit bothered. Seconds later she was pushing the compact into my hands.

'I got ten pound on that one, but you can have it for five.' She winked.

Ryan searched his pockets; I knew he didn't have a tenner on him anyway. Finding five pounds in coins, he handed them over, and the compact was mine.

'It's beautiful,' I told him. 'Thankyou.'

A souvenir of the day. Its value increased instantly.

****

The door to the flats swung open and crashed into the wall. There was a hole in the plaster from it doing this a hundred times before. In fact, the whole hallway was looking a lot more battered and scratched from the last time we were here. We were led into the flat and the familiar brightness from the sun shining in, and heavy smell of paint greeted us.

'Just as we left it.' I thought.

As we went through, I began picking out everything that was wrong with it- as if I had no desperate interest in the place at all.

But I reasoned that no one else seemed to want it, it had been advertised for months now. So, I had the breathing room. Ryan nodded along knowingly, although could tell he was thinking – 'What the fuck is she doing?!'

As the tour came to an end, I told the estate agent we were interested, but not at the asking price. We needed at least £100 off the monthly rent. He didn't question me instead getting straight on the phone to the landlord.

'How did you know to do that?' Ryan whispered to me.

'I didn't.' I shrugged.

He grinned at me, impressed by the boldness of it.

I knew that we were at least £100 short on the current fees, so maybe with a price reduction we'd be able to do it. No one else wanted it- and surely, it was better to have someone in for cheaper than no one in at all.

While the guy was on the phone, I sat on the windowsill and let the sunlight warm my back.

Please be ours. I wished. Please. *I just want somewhere to call home.*

The estate agent came back into the room, clapped his hands together and aid 'The landlord will knock £50 the rent. That's as low as he is willing to go.'

We thanked him and asked when we could apply for it.

I fought back the excitement. It wasn't ours yet.

He said there was another couple due to view it on Monday, but if we paid the fees now, we could have it taken off the market there and then. We followed him up to the agency and paid £250 to secure it. It felt like we were spending a small fortune.

Now, we wait.

We drove back to Bodmin, ready to talk to Mum about it. The money we'd paid was non-refundable, so if our credit rating didn't check out – we'd lose that money. And we were stressed about the credit rating, because we'd been on skid row for so long, we were in debt with Ryan's phone company, by at least £200 now. Would that show up? Would they keep the fees and tell us to get lost?

Also, reading the paperwork through I realised, even though we'd paid the fees, and had it taken off the market, if someone else turned out, paid the fees, paid the deposit and the months' rent up front. It would be theirs, and we'd still lose our money.

It was a whole new load of things to stress about.

Chapter 23 – A Lifetime Later...

This was it. We'd done it.

On Friday 13th September 2013, I took the train over the border into Cornwall for the last time. My diary ended as I sat on that train. I kept the train ticket, slotted in the pages. A reminder, of a journey I never want to repeat.

I collected the keys to the beginning of our new life, and walked into our new home with nothing but the clothes I stood up in. I wandered through the rooms, despite there being nothing new to see, with a quiet excitement. This was it.

What more solid foundation could we begin to rebuild on, than rock bottom?

God, it had been hard. It amused me that friends and acquaintances would lament about the things they had gained through 'hard work.'

'Oh, I've worked hard for this.' They say, about their mortgage or their car or their bonus from their job.

But we worked hard too. Everyone does, I think. Some people just don't seem to work the right 'kind' of hard. My friends worked hard to match the contribution their parents gave them to their deposit.

They worked hard in their office jobs to afford their financed cars.

They worked really hard for that bonus, at Christmas. But the cleaner at their job hadn't gotten a bonus. She mustn't have worked hard enough, I guess.

And us? We'd worked the wrong kind of hard, surviving the days and trying to play our cards right just so that maybe, maybe we could carve out a new start for ourselves.

It had been hard. But to someone who has never struggled it may look like we didn't work hard at all.

Not like them.

It truly is a privilege to be able to work so hard and reap a further reward than basic shelter, and food.

Anyway...

Ryan drove the car to the flat the evening that we moved in, bringing with him an old sofa he'd found for free at work. It took just one trip from the car to take all our worldly belongings into the flat.

The 'new' sofa was a state, but it was something to sit on, and as we sat in the darkness, because the flat didn't come with lightbulbs, I realised that life really wasn't about where we were going, or how hard we were or weren't working, or what things we had. It was who I had doing it with me.

Of course, the adventure didn't end there.

It had only just begun. I found a job, waitressing for an old couple who were quite old fashioned and more often - downright mean. They waved me off at Christmas, promising to see me in January, only when I arrived for my first shift in the New Year, there was a sign on the door telling me they'd retired.

More shit luck, I shrugged. I'd work harder next time.

We could, for the first time, apply for help from the government. We fit the criteria for benefits, although found it often plunged us back into poverty at the whim of the employees' sanction-happy fingers, at the job centre. Thankfully, we lived opposite, so I was never late for an appointment. But after a 6 week wait for any money in the bank, I found I'd be sanctioned for being 15 minutes late to a jobseeker's appointment.

It wasn't true, but with no evidence to prove otherwise, I couldn't fight my corner. Another system I had no idea how to navigate, and that I had promised was a safety net but appeared to be anything but.

Thankfully the lady who ran the antiques shop had become very friendly over the next few weeks. I'd smoke with her and chat. When we managed to save up to buy a proper electric kettle, instead of using the camping stove one, I'd offer her hot drinks – as she couldn't get to the sink in the overfilled shop.

She was an avid scratch card buyer and would buy reams of the tickets at once. Winning a few quid here and there kept her interested. She won £500 one afternoon and I heard her shriek from inside the flat.

On the afternoon of our benefits sanction, we had no food to eat, and no money for two more weeks. We were up that creek without a paddle again. A familiar place by now! Quietly fretting about it, I'd mentioned it to Annette and a few hours later, she'd cashed in a winning card and gave me £20.

'I might be skint, but I'll always share what I 'ave got.' She told me. Pressing the money and three cigarettes into my hand. 'I don't like to think of you going without...'

'I can't take this Annie, it's too much.'

'No, you're having it. You need it more than me right now.' She smiled her toothy grin.

A few months later, I'd found a more secure cleaning job at a hotel, and bumped into Annette ('I hate being called Annie!' She told me, over again.). Things were rough for her lately; she'd found herself in debt with her council tax and her father wasn't well. Annette wasn't young herself, so I imagined her father was fucking ancient.

I walked to the nearest cash point, withdrew £50 and gave it to her. It was half my weeks wage, but the bills were paid, and it was spare.

'I can't 'ave that!' She argued. But I wouldn't take no for an answer.

****

A year later, and things had settled.

Ryan had a steady job, with a Christmas bonus, and even a cut of beef for our festive dinner! We mused about the first Christmas we had in the flat, selling the car to afford the food, tree and presents. Now we had food going spare!

Life had gotten busy again, as it does.

It was a long way from the loneliness and the feelings of being forgotten I'd had sat in the car, whiling the hours away until Ryan got back.

We'd gone to dinner with some friends, and driven back into Plymouth, along the roads we'd driven all the months before, terrified we'd be caught.

As we turned a corner, I spotted a tiny green car parked outside a block of flats.

'Ryan! That looks like-'

As I spoke, we got closer, and I could make out the number plate. That didn't look like our old home. It was the same car.

'I thought you sold it for scrap?!'

'I did!' Ryan laughed. 'At least, I thought I did. The guy told me he could offer scrapping prices, because it was so old...'

'Well, clearly not..!'

We laughed then, because it didn't matter. Look at us now, back in nice clothes and splashing out on a posh meal. It didn't matter.

I thought about it often, living in that car. As we quietly stepped back into normal life, and felt a serene bliss about it all. It had been worth it. Every scary moment. Every slight despair.

We'd grown into lives that fit us, and when we walked along the beaches, in the winter when everyone else had to go back home, to their 'real lives'. We were still here. Winter sun on our backs, the sound of the waves licking the shore.

Seagulls had become the background noise to our life now, adventure had become a weekly occurrence as we explored somewhere new, somewhere that no ghosts would be found. It was ours now.

And we had never felt so free.

After Thoughts.....

Of course, the story didn't end there...!

We went back to Dad's after settling into our new life. To gather the last of our things, although Dad had gotten rid of most of it. All those tiny sentimental things I thought I'd always have time to fetch, gone in a moment.

But again, it is only stuff. The real sentiment is in the things we feel, and do. Not held up in a ratty old teddy, or a photograph. No ticket stub really holds the memory of what you did when you got there.

Dad and I never mentioned our falling out, it was all swept under the rug. I figured there would be plenty of time to ask him why, or apologise for my own behaviour. He wasn't well, and he knew it. He will be well again one day, I hope. Amends are made silently sometimes; we don't need a big fanfare to heal us. Quiet healing counts too.

For Dad, it was in the cup of tea he made us, when we returned after a year. For Mum, it was coming to see us, sending us money when we needed it. Asking no questions, just quietly offering a hand up – not a handout.

Looking back at it all, and remembering what we went through is just astonishing. Do I regret it?

Not one bit.

Sure, we could have planned it a bit better, we could have saved up and found jobs and set ourselves up ready – but really – would we have still made it? Was that even a possibility for us? It didn't feel like it, and that's why we didn't do that.

Are we happy now?

Happiness has become my default setting. I wake up each morning in disbelief – I'm still here. I am so lucky. I made it.

And yes, many people look in at my life and might decide it not up to their standard, but here is the most wonderful thing I have learned of all – I don't care.

I am so truly content with what I have I don't wish a single day away. I don't care for the lottery, and I don't count down the days until 'the holiday starts.'

Happiness is attainable. It isn't a pipe dream; it won't spirit you away.

So dear reader, go. Do good things.

Help people that are worse off than you.

If you are unhappy, then re-evaluate. Do something that scares you, because something wonderful waits on the other side.

Make a life that makes you happy when it's quiet and there's no one around. When winter sets in, when the beach is empty. Make that your life.

It is possible.

Acknowledgements.

I did it. I got to the end. And you did too, if you are reading this. So, my first thanks to you, dear reader. For getting to the end.

My next thanks, of course, spoiler alert – goes to my wonderful husband, Ryan. For believing in me when no one else did. For pushing me every day to write the diary in the first place. For listening with your eyes shut when we were there, in that car. No idea what the future held. For making that car feel like home, simply by being there with me.

Thank you for then pushing me further, to get it written, to edit it and make something of it all. I wouldn't have done this, if not for you. I love you.

My second thanks goes to my lovely followers, on Facebook, Instagram, on my blog, in the street. Thank you for believing in me also, for following my journey and all its highs and lows. For asking for advice, and then giving it in spades.

For all of you who have checked in when I've been quiet. The world needs more of you. Don't ever feel like you have gone unnoticed. You haven't, and now here you have a whole paragraph dedicated to you. Thankyou.

Next of course, although he will never get to read this, my Dad. I miss you every day. I loved you more than I realised, and you loved me in return. Thank you for being a wonderful Daddy, and I forgive you for the times you weren't. The life lesson you really taught me was that we are all human. And humans are flawed. And that is ok. Thankyou.

Mum, of course I wouldn't leave you out of my book. Thank you for always coming back.

To Ryan's Mum and Dad, who I love more than I think they know. Thank you for being there. Thank you for all the love. Thankyou for giving me Ryan.

Nanny and Grandad, aka Hazel and Pat. Thankyou for the laughs. For the cups of tea and visits. Thankyou.

To Danielle, at Brand13, thank you for saving my book cover at the eleventh hour! I will never use paint again!

To Hannah Ewins, formerly Stowe. For letting me use your name when I get in trouble, except when we were in trouble together, which was A LOT. Thankyou for being my wonderful best friend.

To all our friends, I'm sorry I can't list you all, I'd only forget one of you and find myself off the Christmas card list, which is more than I could bear! But thank you for loving us, when we disappeared without a trace, when we felt misguided about life, when we hid our truth from you all and worried you all silly. We are back now! And we love you all, so much.

To the man with the pasta, Matt and his strange note, the kind security guy, the man and the bus ticket, the policeman that let us off and most importantly for Sarah, if that was your name, because I am never sure if I even imagined you up. Thank you for being the difference in this world. Thank you for going above and beyond to be kind, decent people. For restoring the faith, and reminding me, especially, that there are many humans on this planet who really are just kind. Thankyou for proving that random acts of kindness are really huge parts of humanity.

Each one of you replenished my now unwavering optimism about life.

Thankyou.

Thankyou.

Thankyou.

Printed in Great
Britain
by Amazon